Waiting at the Window

A Guide to Deeper Prayer

Sharon Riddle

You will find that the best way to read this book is to read until you feel inspired to pray. Then, set the book down and do it. Even if you never finish the book you will not miss its treasure.

Copyright © 2003 by Sharon Riddle

Waiting at the Window
by Sharon Riddle

Printed in the United States of America

ISBN 0-9761583-1-0

All rights reserved. No part of this publication may be reproduced or transmitted in any form or by any means without written permission of the publisher.

Unless otherwise indicated, Bible quotations are taken from the New American Standard Bible. Copyright © 1989-1996 by The Lockman Foundation.

Olive Leaf Publications
www.oliveleafpublications.com

Olive Leaf Publications are distributed through Lightning Source, Inc.,
and on the Web at www.oliveleafpublications.com

Acknowledgments

My thanks

- To Terry, Jean, Lowell, Michelle and Dick, for their editorial abilities.

- To my husband Ike for being a man of prayer even when *no one* is looking.

- To my daughters Beth and Mary (my intense love for them makes me *lean* on Him)

- To my mother, who taught me to pray, and my father, who taught me to dream.

- To my Olive Branch family for permission to let their lives illustrate these pages.

Table of Contents

Aknowledgments v
Prologue ix

1. Learning to Pray 11
2. Fighting in an Invisible Arena 33
3. Witnessing God Projects 45
4. Paying Back the Enemy 71
5. Dealing with Hurt 79
6. Praying Prayers That Get Answered 105
7. Walking by the Spirit's Guidance
   Through Prayer 119
8. Experiencing True Faith 139
9. Waiting on God 167
10. Warring through Prayer 187
11. Exercising Humility in Prayer 211
12. Learning to Fear the Lord 231

Epilogue 243

Prologue

The adventure of deeper prayer is available to every Christian, regardless of how long they have walked with God. Many times throughout the days and nights God calls to us, His beloved, to "Come away with Me." And with His song of love wafting in through the window of our activity, He woos us. Many hear the music, few respond. Their desires and schedules have a deafening effect, drowning out the song and muddling it up with motion.

Unfortunately, hurt and difficulty are most likely the mentors who will finally urge us to kneel at His feet. These master teachers know how to shut the doors of distraction and open the perception of our own helplessness. They help produce the first embryonic cries or groans of deeper prayer.

Then, with time, we discover THE PEARL, that deeper prayer is absolutely essential to our existence. One by one we cast aside our temporal treasures to procure it. With a farewell to everything others call "life," we welcome and embrace it.

If you decide to sing the Master's song with Him you will learn to wait by the window. Many times you will pause in the midst of a task and look out, hoping to catch a glimpse of His form. You will experience pain as you long for His presence. But in the waiting you will hear the voice that carries "full joy" in its sound. You will be the invited guest who reclines at the table of rich delights that satisfy the pangs of hunger. You will hear your name called often when the Master wishes for a servant and you will leap with ecstasy when He empowers you to the task.

Waiting at the window, you will many times find that He has left something of Himself there for you to hold. It bears His fragrance. It fills the room until His next visit. I hope you will join me at the window.

1

Learning To Pray?

The desire to pray

There are many people who would **like** to pray more. Unfortunately, many view prayer like they view broccoli. They universally promote the benefits of eating it, but rarely taste its delights. Some are frustrated because they don't know **how** to get into the habit of prayer. They have no consistency in their devotional life. There are no patterns (however simple in nature) to their well-digging in God's Word through which inspiration naturally springs up and refreshes. Others don't know how to get beyond their **habits** to **habitation** in the presence of God. There must be growth from **discipline** to **delight** if we are ever to truly hunger and thirst for righteousness, **and thereby receive the fulfillment of the promise** *to be filled.* However, just having the "want to" to pray more is a good place to begin. This is where the disciples stood when they said "Lord, teach us to pray."

"If man is man and God is God, to live without prayer is

not merely an awful thing: it is an infinitely foolish thing."
Phillips Brooks, 19th century pastor

Don't just hang around prayer, learn to pray

Cooking and praying are alike in this way: Some people hang around the kitchen but never learn to cook. Many who make up the churches of our day fool themselves into thinking that they cook. Take a look at today's church potlucks (if you can find one). They are stocked with grocery store and deli containers, fast-food chicken and pre-frozen casseroles. Sadly, we think our microwave prayers are satisfying enough also.

Recently a friend invited women from our church to learn to bake with Phyllo dough. It's a time consuming process of painting thin sheets of pastry with butter. We made little packets of cheese and spinach. We also nestled apples and cinnamon in a tasty streusel. While we were buttering the tender dough, God was softening up our hearts to each other. We shared heartaches, as well as pastry brushes. The result was a fabulous taste sensation that could never have come out of a freezer. The body of Christ ate a meal dripping with love and fellowship that day and our families now eat fabulously due to our newfound skills. In a similar way, Christ beckons us into His kitchen. The delights that await us there are far beyond what we have experienced so far. There will be an adventure of peeling back layers and layers of "you" and ladling in layers and layers of "Him." But in the end, God's creation will be sensational. The full flavor He wants us to enjoy could never have been zapped into us in a process of minutes.

Connection with God

You must be one who honestly desires to climb the

heights of intimacy with God (or you wouldn't be reading this). But so far you may have spent a lot of time simply walking around the foothills. In order to experience the panoramic view of deep prayer, we must realize that the first and basic premise of prayer is that we need to have a real **connection** with the Lord Jesus Christ. As we experience the true vine/branch relationship, (John 15), as we see the supernatural power of God at work through our prayers and as the Almighty breathes on us through His Word, we will naturally begin to want more *grain* and less *straw*. Straw is what we see accomplished through our own human efforts. Grain is what we experience when our humanness is overshadowed by the power of God. It is well beyond anything we could ever think up or imagine, and it is so effective, so different in nature from what we have ever experienced through our own futile methods, that it is its own reward. It leads us naturally on the uphill trail of wanting more of Jesus. It conditions our soul for the higher altitude and we long to linger above, not below. The higher we climb the better the view we enjoy, and this makes us look for encouragement to those who have gone ahead of us. They call out "come up higher" and we know that we must.

"If we would pray aright, the first thing we should do is to see to it that we really get an audience with God, that we really get into His very presence. Before a word of petition is offered, we should have the definite consciousness that we are talking to God, and should believe that He is listening and is going to grant the thing that we ask of Him." Dr. R.A. Torrey

It is possible to miss a vital connection with the living God for many years. People come to God and accept His gift of salvation, but they can be blind to the living, breathing connection they have with Him. In discipling a young woman, I felt the Holy Spirit indicate that this was where she needed to grow. We spent the good portion of a discipleship session talking about being "connected" to Jesus and making our prayer time grow out of that premise, not that of fulfilling an obligation. I got an email a few days later saying that she was beginning to experience this connected relationship in her time with the Lord. Later in the week she mentioned that she had received an answer to prayer. Her excitement was growing! Then a week later I had to cancel our time together. This was because a marriage-counseling situation with a couple from church required both my husband and me to facilitate. My friend told me that during her prayer time the Lord had laid on her heart the desire to watch my children for me during the counseling session. This was how I knew she was "getting the point" of our precious lesson. She was now experiencing true relationship with God. She was beyond a rote exercise of devotion. The Lord could communicate His desires to her and she was communicating her desires to Him. This is where real prayer begins.

Hurt and trials help us to pray more

Unfortunately, usually trial and heartache are the tutors that lead us to new levels in prayer. They are the most effective at getting our attention and convincing us of our need. The pointers of pain tap us on our heads and we find ourselves listening more attentively to the Scriptural principles the Lord is writing out on the blackboard of our hearts. For the treasure they bring us, for the lifetime of reward they endow, we must be grateful for their role in our lives. We can return to the classrooms of spiritual learning years later for a reunion of rejoicing and thank our loving Lord for using such gruff, stern taskmasters to teach us the fundamental truth of abiding in Him.

In my own life there had always been *prayer*, but in the spring of 1999 the Lord used some heartbreaking events in the church where my husband is the pastor, to get my attention and draw me deeper on the journey. That year had been particularly difficult. Several families had experienced unresolved conflict and left. Our church morale was at one of its lowest ebbs and I was desperate to see healing. As my husband and I lay on our faces before God Most High and implored His hand to help us, I remember saying something like this to Him, "I don't want anymore emotional carnage to be a result of **my** *prayer-little-ness*." I was having a consistent quiet time, but because we were in a state of all out spiritual war it was necessary to allow the Lord to take me to a deeper level of prayer. At that time I made a commitment to the Lord. I told Him that if He would wake me in the middle of the night, I would get up and spend no less than two hours with Him. The bulk of the responsibility lay on Him. He would have to waken me out of a deep sleep. My only responsibility would be that once I was awake, I would get up and give Him the time I had promised. (It is important to note that before this time I always slept "through the night." Except for the seasons of pregnancy, I had been a sound sleeper.) The Lord has been faithful to wake me and even to help me keep my commitment to Him. In direct response to our cry for help and guidance, the Lord has used this time with Him to revolutionize our lives and methods for ministry. As your Creator, the Lord knows the amount of time you need for rest. He also can wake you to be used for His purposes. When you begin to trust His ability to do this you will see what I mean.

More time for prayer

If you want to go deeper with the Lord you must allow Him to STRETCH the time you are used to spending in His presence. Wherever you are right now in your prayer life, you can find a new place in Him simply by committing more time to be with Him. It is important to use wisdom in setting new goals for your time with the Lord. If up to now you have only prayed for say, fifteen minutes a day, it would not be prudent to jump to a goal of four hours a day. With the Lord's help, commit a reasonable period of time that you believe you can, be consistent in fulfilling. It is not necessary to have your prayer time in the middle of the night to become a man or woman of prayer. However, if you are determined to be used greatly in the work of intercession, it is almost a given that you will be giving a portion of your sleep time to Him. During the night is when much spiritual activity takes place.

I thank the Lord for the privilege of being awakened at all different times to accomplish His purposes. Sometimes I will wake up only two or three hours after I have gone to sleep. Many times the Lord shakes me to consciousness at about two or three in the morning. And then the Lord sometimes wakes me exactly two hours before I have to get up for some event or duty. When the Lord is done with me many times I go back to bed and am able to feel completely rested the next morning. I don't want to give the impression, however, that I am never tired during my time with the Lord. I find that sleepiness is a spiritual war tactic of the enemy that can be fought with perseverance, a cup of tea and walking. It is encouraging to note that when Jesus prayed in the night He was ALSO tired. Otherwise He wouldn't have been found sleeping in the boat during the storm. When Jesus fasted, he felt hunger. There is no place of obedience that His sandals have not tread upon before ours. He can help us on our way.

"And He came to the disciples and found them sleeping, and said to Peter, 'So, you men could not keep watch with Me for one hour?'" Matthew 26:40

Learning To Pray?

On several occasions when weariness seemed insurmountable I have cried out to the Lord for His help and continued "gutting it out" in obedience. In response, the Lord has pointed out a new insight in His Word or at other times He has allowed me to enjoy His presence in a new way. God was answering my heart's desire with more of Himself. Meditate on the following verses that express the desire to experience a new place of intimacy with God and then ask Him to take you to a new "face to face" place with Him.

"The secret of the Lord is for those who fear Him, and He will make them know His covenant." Psalm 25:14

"When Thou didst say, 'Seek My face,' my heart said to Thee, 'Thy face, O Lord, I shall seek.'" Psalm 27:8

"No man can do a great and enduring work for God who is not a man of prayer, and no man can be a man of prayer who does not give much time to praying." E.M. Bounds, <u>Power Through Prayer</u>*, p. 40-41.*

Deeper prayer

One thing I have learned about myself over the years: no matter how busy I am, I am always busy enough to avoid housework. I vacuum once a week, usually on the day when the women come to my home for Bible study. Then one day I was introduced to a special kind of vacuum cleaner. A woman convinced me to endure her *sales pitch* and I was truly amazed by what I saw. Over and over a filter was put into the vacuum that captured the dirt *my* vacuum had missed. Again and again the filter was filled and discarded. I could suddenly see that what I had called *vacuuming* and what this woman considered *vacuuming* were two very different things. There was no comparison.

This is similar to what happened in my life in the area of prayer. I had always "prayed." But the day came when God began to teach me more about prayer, what *He* considered *praying*, and there was no comparison. His teaching took me deeper into the fibers of spirituality than my "surface" praying had ever gone.

"You can read all the manuals on prayer and listen to other people pray, but until you begin to pray yourself you will never understand prayer. It's like riding a bicycle or swimming: You learn by doing." Evangelist Luis Palau

Equipped to pray

When we want to grow in prayer we must be equipped to pray. We can *always* pray *anytime* and *anywhere* without *anything*, (without special tools), but I have found several things *helpful* to have in my time with Him. The first is **a place to pray**. It should be a consistent place (except when you are away from home). For my mother it was a rocking chair in our living room. I found her there almost every morning when I got up. She would be sitting with her Bible on her lap, a cup of tea and a box of tissues nearby. Many times there were tears of joy or intercession on her face. How my heart listened to the sermon she preached on those days! She loved Him and longed to be in His presence, and I know that although her armor was only a robe, she was entrenched in warring for our family from the vantagepoint of that comfy little chair.

When I go on retreats and trips, I find that choosing a "place of prayer" can be a real adventure. At one retreat I regularly attend I have to walk in the dark quite a distance to get a place "apart" from others. One night as I made my way in the dark of night and crossed a grassy patch on the way to the Prayer Chapel I was suddenly hit by automatic sprinklers.

Learning To Pray?

After that event I began asking God in advance to help prepare the details of where and how I would pray when I am away from home.

At another camp the staff had experienced quite a bit of BEAR traffic. I got to a new place of trust by believing God to clear them away as I made my way alone in the dark to the place where there was warmth and solitude. He did it. Although I would sometimes hear the rattle of trash cans OUTSIDE while I prayed, I never saw a bear and never had one disturb my safe passage to and from the cabin.

I have also found that it is helpful to have several tools available. I keep blank 3x5 cards handy. These I use to write out verses the Lord impresses on me while reading His Word. I write out the verse and note the main subject in the right hand corner. Then these are filed so that in the future when I want to find a particular verse, I can. (Sometimes the Lord reminds me of things I need to do later in the day and I use the cards to write these down so I can put them out of my mind during the remainder of my quiet time.) I also keep a pen handy for writing notes in my Bible, several colored highlighters, paper clips and rubber bands (I group verse cards by subject and this keeps them together), my Bible, file boxes for verse cards, and my prayer notebook with requests, answers and dates. Nearby is always a box of tissues too. You never know when you will need that. *Caution: You can have all this equipment and still not reach a new place in prayer.*

Garden prayer

I grew up in a pastor's home and from a young age felt a natural ease in talking to God. I remember wandering in the basement of our house, which doubled as Sunday School rooms, and talking out loud to the Lord. Other times a little orchard that bordered our property became a place of walking and talking with God. In my college days, God and I had marvelous times of fellowship sharing dreams and loving thoughts. We walked across the spacious campus. There was a **natural delight** in sharing things with my Creator. This kind of praying I call "garden praying." No doubt this is the kind of praying that Adam and Eve experienced as they joined God in the cool of the evening. It is just conversation about everything and anything that might have crossed my path during the previous day.

This is where my time with God begins each day. I unload worries onto His broad shoulders. I recognize the stains of sin and allow His laundry service to make me white as snow. I throw out little fishing lines of faith that begin with "Lord, wouldn't it be great if today was the day *so and so* came to know you as their Lord?" or "Father, could you please give me a special time of Your presence today?" "Would you please honor us with revival?" Many times God gives a little tug on the other end and we begin the process over hours, weeks, months or years of reeling His perfect will up onto the surface of reality. These experiences have made me a fisherman for life.

Have you ever seen the fishing game at a carnival? I remember a scene in the movie *Pollyanna* where Polly expressed her dream for a doll to an older woman. Polly was the daughter of a missionary, and she would anxiously await the "barrels" that would bring second hand things to them from across the ocean. She hoped that her request would be answered, but the doll never arrived. This same woman was with Polly at the fishing game, and watched the person behind the wall pick out a prize to put on the end of the young girl's fishing line. The carnival worker started to hang a different prize on the line, but the older woman shook her head to indicate that the doll was what Polly really wanted. Sometimes I think that these "hearts desires" prayers of ours cause our Heavenly Father to let us snag and later hold the things we long for most. He has laid up many blessings and possibilities to delight us, but as we dream out loud in our prayers, He picks up the things we ask for (prepared beforehand by His grace) and ties them onto our line.

The Chinese symbol for happiness is a man in a garden.

List prayer

Another kind of praying is important if we are to grow in prayer. This is "list praying." It requires keeping a list of our requests and the answers to prayer that the Lord gives. In my prayer notebook I enter a request and the date I began praying about it. When the prayer is answered I also enter the date. This list is now so many pages long that I cannot pray over the whole list each day, so I have to set a certain number of pages that I pray over each day. When I come to a prayer request that was answered, I always stop to thank the Lord for His goodness. When an answer comes to a question of God's will (whether it was a yes, no or wait), I thank Him for His great wisdom and love that have protected and guided me.

The value of list praying is that it helps us pray for things beyond our capacity to remember. When people ask me to pray about something, if it doesn't get put on this list, it is soon forgotten. One year I taught a prayer seminar at an Association of Christian Schools International Convention. At the conclusion I invited people to fill out a prayer request card. After almost a year of praying over those cards, I did some phone calling to see what the Lord was doing over these requests. I found surprising answers. One woman had asked me to pray for her husband who was ill at the time. About six months after my commitment to pray for him they had changed insurance carriers and doctors. He was immediately diagnosed by the new doctor and, with the appropriate diagnosis and treatment, was well on the road to recovery. Another woman had requested prayer for students in her class. When I called to find out their progress it was after the school year had ended. I will never forget her delight as she told me that every single one of them had improved! Praise the Lord! If I hadn't kept a list I would have never remembered the people or their requests by that time.

"In the morning, O Lord, Thou wilt hear my voice; in the morning I will order my prayer to Thee and eagerly watch." Psalm 5:3

Distractions to prayer

If you have your quiet time in the middle of the night, usually the only distractions you face are internal, such as a wandering attention or sleepiness. If you have it during the day the distractions you will face will be *internal and external* (like people needing your attention, telephone calls or changes in schedule/activity). If you are easily distracted or your house is especially hectic you may want to schedule your quiet time when the rest of the family members are asleep. (Note: People are more alert at different times in the day. Find the time that you are most focused and alert and carve out an island of prayer.)

"The morning watch is essential. You must not face the day until you have faced God, nor look into the face of others until you have looked into His." Mrs. Charles Cowman, Streams in the Desert, p. 7

When we begin to pray, the enemy's first defense will be to try to make us think about any other little thing that needs to be done. He will try to wean us away from the presence of God as quickly as possible. Years ago our church performed a drama that illustrated this point. A young woman who had committed to pray for one hour was reminded, by *demonic imps,* to cut out name tags for her daughter's field trip and to iron the shirt her husband would need for work. As she, in obedience continued to pray, she found that the distraction of these trivial matters was forgotten and when her hour was finally up, and she COULD take care of them, the mental battle was over. There was no longer a force pulling her to complete them, and she went back to bed confident that there would be enough time in the morning to get them all done.

This drama illustrates an important point. The only time some things will seem important is when the enemy is trying to keep you from the MOST IMPORTANT activity. The easiest way to combat his tactics is to make a commitment not to do anything else before you have your prayer time. It is sacred time. There is nothing our powerful God can't help us attend to after we have attended to His worship and presence.

Prayer with small children around

When I had children, I began to repent of my judgmental attitudes towards women who were not powerful in prayer and Bible study. For years I had faced these tired moms with the compassion of a drill sergeant and in my heart had expressed disdain for their complacent attitudes towards God. When I had children of my own, I discovered what a battle it was. I am still convinced though, that it is a battle worth fighting. Like many other activities that little ones make challenging, i.e. cleaning house, preparing meals, we just have to keep picking at the things we value most. After all, we don't give up putting on our makeup, doing yard work, or wearing clean clothes because we have children. We just prioritize and plan ahead what really must get done. The same can be done with our time with God.

Picking away at the important things

There are many tasks in life that seem overwhelming. If we could see them in their totality we would be too discouraged to even begin. However, "picking" away at them completes many of these jobs. When we moved into our home, eight years ago, it was a mess. It had sat for over a year with no inhabitants and all the landscape had gone *out of control*. My husband, a farmer boy from Tennessee, began picking away at the task of trimming, weeding and fertilizing. I have two memorable pictures of our house that hang right next to my computer. One shows a dull brown house with no lawn (it all had to be dug up and reseeded). The other shows a bright and cheery cream colored house with lots and lots of beautiful flowers all around it. I like to use these two pictures to give people hope for their lives.

We never had a lot of money to fix up our house. We just took care of what we saw we could do as we lived in it. One time a man in our church brought some rose plants to our house that were to be thrown away at his work. They made a big difference. Then my parents helped us purchase a new garage door. A couple of men from church helped us paint. There were many weeks the trashcans were brimming with clippings. And over time what a difference this "picking" has made in our house. Your life might be a mess right now, habits of prayer might be overgrown with the cares of life. But as Phil. 3:21 tells us, wherever Jesus lives it's going to end up looking beautiful, like Him. His power is able to transform our lives into conformity with His glory. So just start *picking away* at getting more prayer in your life.

Running away with God

There are times throughout the day when you will hear the Lord calling you to "run away with Him" for more prayer. As you respond to His invitation, you will find this kind of prayer to be very satisfying. It's love in its purest form. Wanting to be in His presence when you don't "have to" for any reason other than fellowship and intimacy brings you to a new place with God Almighty and you will find His ears surprisingly open to your heart's cry. (Just like your husband or wife would be if you asked to spend a little time with them in the middle of the day—*just because you love them so much.*)

When our church began to look for land on which to build, my husband began praying on a parcel that he believed would be just right for us. I soon followed suit and as I walked around its perimeter I prayed that God would do what He had promised the Israelites, *that every place the sole of their feet tread would be theirs.* In my dusty hiking boots I cried out to the Lord to make this deserted and desolate corner a place for His glory, and that He would place a LIGHT in this area of heavy crime and economic neediness. One day I even found what looked like a little altar, no doubt erected for no good purpose, in the middle of the property. I got the feeling Gideon might have experienced as I kicked the stones apart and consecrated the land for the worship of the Lord Most High alone. Many people were praying for our church to have a place to call home. We had agreed together about this over a long period of time. But I know that a part of the victory in prayer came from the many times I ran away with God and dreamed with Him about the potential of this place.

Later, armed with very limited funds, we began the process of trying to purchase this piece of property. To the glory and honor of God our Father, on the final day of escrow a large gift came in that paid for the land in cash and made the need for a huge loan obsolete. This meant that our funds could be put towards constructing a building instead. Again and again the neighbors probably noticed cars that would occasionally drive up and park on this vacant lot. They would see a person slip out and walk around the land, get back in the car and drive away. They never knew that like the surveying walk of Nehemiah, a spiritual evaluation was taking place, resources were being stockpiled and the enemy was being pressed back. All of it was done in quiet times of prayer.

During the construction of our building, over 2 million dollars was given towards the work, AND shortly before the building was completed the Lord gave us an additional gift of more land and a center for our youth. (A gift of two hundred eighty-five thousand dollars!) The Lord provided a 4.2 million-dollar project to our church with only a 1.6 million-dollar loan commitment. He also helped us refinance the loan after one year to cut years off the payments. You never know what God will do when you slip away to be with Him!

"But He Himself would often slip away to the wilderness and pray." Luke 5:16

Let the Lord manage your time

In December of 2002, I saw again how reverence for the Lord added hours to the day. There always seems to be too much to do in our lives. Putting the Lord's work behind our own desires and pleasures is a constant temptation. I was frantically trying to prepare for a Christmas Eve service by writing instrumental arrangements, preparing chapel music for our school, wrapping presents, etc. On one specific day the Lord called on me to set aside some special time to pray with a woman I had never met. An internal struggle ended when I submitted to be God's true servant.

Later in the day I drove to the mall to get a box of See's candy for my mother-in-law. The Lord opened up the FIRST parking space by the door, this was just a few days before Christmas! In addition to that, as I stopped at the post office, I had a friend give me his number and only had to wait 10 min. (This particular post office is understaffed and even without the Christmas rush you can have a LONG wait.) So don't worry that you have too much to do to pray.

It's like the illustration of the rice and walnuts. If you put 2 cups of rice into a Mason jar and then try to add 2 cups of walnuts, they won't fit. But if you put in the walnuts first (God's priorities), the rice will fit also.

We know that every single person who has ever lived has had the same 24 hours a day to spend. But some have spent them more wisely than others. Some have left an indelible mark on the world and others have frittered away their potential. It all happens as we make the daily decisions of what will go in the jar first. That's why the Lord is perfectly suited to help us. After all, He created the whole universe in just six days. He has already promised in His Word that He is available and willing to help us. He is also able to teach us, like He taught Martha, what things should automatically go at the top of the list.

"But Martha was distracted with all her preparations; and she came up to Him, and said, 'Lord, do You not care that my sister has left me to do all the serving alone? Then tell her to help me.' But the Lord answered and said to her, 'Martha, Martha, you are worried and bothered about so many things; but only a few things are necessary, really only one, for Mary has chosen the good part, which shall not be taken away from her.'" Luke 10:40-42

Good or best

Satan is an artist at distracting us from the best things with a wagonload of good things. God's people face hundreds of opportunities for service each week. The more we grow in prayer, the more we discover the truth that prayer can motivate a hundred hearts to a task. But sometimes in our prayer the Lord finds He only needs one to do His work, us. The wonderful thing about a life wholly submitted to the Lord in prayer is that God knows how to fulfill us without exhausting us. He knows, like the perfect personal trainer would, just what kinds of exercises will help and how much we need to stretch without breaking. When opportunities come up we don't always know "right off" what God's will is. Therefore we have to ask and listen. Because guilt and selfishness can yell as loudly as conviction, we have to seek the Lord's face and wait for His response. Isn't it interesting that as the disciples matured in their walk that they left "waiting on tables" for the more necessary prayer and the Word? But lest you think that being deep into prayer turns you into a couch potato, remember that it was Jesus who picked up the towel and washed feet. Prayer simply, like a hearing aid, cuts down on the white noise in the room, so we can hear Him better.

"You yourself can influence more people for God by prayer than in any other way. It is not the only thing you must do, but the greatest thing you can do." Wesley Deuwel

Prayer journal entry:

Note: Dates are taken verbatim from my list. Answers have been edited so that the reader can understand the circumstances of the situation.

9/19/02 Felt great desire to "run away with God" for a special time of prayer after having been inspired by R.A. Torrey's book How to Pray. Unfortunately this was the only day I had to prepare instrumental music for a wedding that would be held the next day. I asked God to "cover" the wedding because I knew that time in His presence would be the best activity to choose.

9/20/02 With just a few minutes to prepare on the day of the wedding, the Lord led me to use several worship songs during the prelude of the wedding. The couple were devoted Christians. I knew the worship tunes already and was able to experience relaxed worship as I played. Normally I would have been nervous playing music that I only see a couple times a year.

Prayer myth: Only great people can accomplish great things through prayer

Sometimes people look at others and think, "Sure God answers their prayers, but I could never see those kinds of answers." The idea that God loves some of His children more than others is simply not true. He is a just God and this means that in prayer we are all on equal ground. We all have the same opportunities. It is what we do with them that will determine our effectiveness.

*"Prayer is not the mystical experience of a few special people, but an aggressive act- an act that may be **performed by anyone** who will accept the challenge to learn to pray."* Jack Hayford

The following verse shows us that it is **not even possible** for God to love some people more than others. The only way to influence Him is through obedience and faith. We are all on level ground in these two areas for we all have a will to submit and hope to enflame. *"For the Lord your God is the God of gods and the Lord of lords, the great, the mighty, and the awesome God **who does not show partiality**, nor take a bribe." Deuteronomy 10:17*

Saturate your prayers with these truths and the treasures they guarantee:

"The upright will behold His face." Psalm 11:7b "Thou wilt make known to me the path of life; in Thy presence is fullness of joy; in Thy right hand there are pleasures forever." Psalm 16:11 "As for me, I shall behold Thy face in righteousness; I will be satisfied with Thy likeness when I awake." Psalm 17:15 "Call to Me, and I will answer you, and I will tell you great and mighty things, which you do not know." Jeremiah 33:3 "He who has My commandments and keeps them, he it is who loves Me; and he who loves Me shall be loved by My Father, and I will love him, and will disclose Myself to him." John 14:21 "But just as it is written, 'Things which eye has not seen and ear has not heard, and which have not entered the heart of man, all that God has prepared for those who love Him.'" I Corinthians 2:9

Question: If God's already determined what He's going to do, why should I pray?

A portion of this statement is true, but the conclusion is false. To help us understand our part in the prayer process, think about the Empire State Building for a moment. There was certainly a tremendous amount of power behind designing and bringing that fine piece of architecture into reality. Yet for a small boy on a tour who puts in a quarter (or whatever it costs these days) to ride the elevator to the top, it is a true statement that he has *had a part* in the process. That's how I feel about my part in prayer. Of course God alone can provide for His work and accomplish His will. However, He lets me put in my little two bits worth (the asking and believing) and then He comes through with the wisdom, the power and the glory and accomplishes His perfect will. I stand at the top of answered prayer requests and look down from a thrilling vantage point and know that although He invited me to participate in the process, He could have chosen to use any one of the other awe-struck visitors to do the same thing.

Read the following verses and meditate on the fact that God wants to construct some awesome accomplishments with you. Stop and spend a period of time dreaming up some skyscrapers of faith with the One that got His reputation from building them.

"If you ask Me anything in My name, I will do it." John 14:14 "And whatever you ask in My name, that will I do, that the Father may be glorified in the Son." John 14:13 "If you abide in Me, and My words abide in you, ask whatever you wish, and it shall be done for you." John 15:7 "Even now I know that whatever You ask of God, God will give You." John 11:22

We read in scripture that our participation **does make a difference** in the outcome of circumstances: *"In those days Hezekiah became mortally ill. And Isaiah the prophet the son of Amoz came to him and said to him, 'Thus says the Lord, "Set your house in order, for you shall die and not live.'" Then Hezekiah turned his face to the wall, and prayed to the Lord, and said, 'Remember now, O Lord, I beseech Thee, how I have walked before Thee in truth and with a whole heart, and have done what is good in Thy sight.' And Hezekiah wept bitterly. Then the word of the Lord came to Isaiah, saying, 'Go and say to Hezekiah, "Thus says the Lord, the God of your father David, **I have heard your prayer**, I have seen your tears; behold, I will add fifteen* *years to your life.' " Isaiah 38:1-5*

"And Ahab said to Elijah, 'Have you found me, O my enemy?' And he answered, 'I have found you, because you have sold yourself to do evil in the sight of the Lord. "Behold, I will bring evil upon you, and will utterly sweep you away, and will cut off from Ahab every male, both bond and free in Israel; and I will make your house like the house of Jeroboam the son of Nebat, and like the house of Baasha the son of Ahijah, because of the provocation with which you have provoked Me to anger, and because you have made Israel sin." And of Jezebel also has the Lord spoken, saying, "The dogs shall eat Jezebel in the district of Jezreel. The one belonging to Ahab, who dies in the city, the dogs shall eat, and the one who dies in the field the birds of heaven shall eat.' " Surely there was no one like Ahab who sold himself to do evil in the sight of the Lord, because Jezebel his wife incited him. And he acted very abominably in following idols, according to all that the Amorites had done, whom the Lord cast out before the sons of Israel. And it came about when Ahab heard these words that, he tore his clothes and put on sackcloth and fasted, and he lay in sackcloth and went about despondently. Then the word of the Lord came to Elijah the Tishbite, saying, 'Do you see how Ahab has humbled himself before Me? Because he has humbled himself before Me, I will not bring the evil in his days, but I will bring the evil upon his house in his son's days.' " I Kings 21:20-29

"To men who think praying their main business...does God commit the keys of his kingdom, and by them does he work his spiritual wonders in this world." E.M. Bounds

2

Fighting In
An Invisible Arena

Not too long ago, we watched a news story that reported about planes, which dropped bombs from such an altitude, that they were unable to see their target. As a result, they were totally dependent on ground forces for the coordinates of where to drop their weapons. In the same way, if you go on to new ground in prayer, you will have to begin to fight on a level where sight is of no advantage. Think of a cartoon where the villain has dipped himself in invisible ink. In order to see the villain it would take goggles designed to negate the effects of the ink. In the physical realm this would be a tremendous invention, but where do we obtain such a marvelous invention for the spiritual realm? It is in prayer. To fight a war of this type there must be an army of people working together and committed to victory. And there must be no unconfessed sin to interfere with the communication we have with the Lord. He can see everything going on in the battle from His omnipresent location. What follows, in prayer, is an intense period of "crying" out to the Lord and then there comes, a sense of peace and fulfillment EVEN BEFORE THE OUTCOME IS CHANGED. Here is an example from God's Word of this kind of prayer.

"Then Samuel said, 'Gather all Israel to Mizpah, and I will pray to the Lord for you.' Then the sons of Israel said to Samuel, **'Do not cease to cry to the Lord our God for us,** *that He may save us from the hand of the Philistines.' And Samuel took a suckling lamb and offered it for a whole burnt offering to the Lord; and* **Samuel cried to the Lord for Israel and the Lord answered him."** *I Samuel 7:5,8 -9*

The Israelites have just received back the Ark of the Covenant, which had been held captive by the Philistines for seven months while God used it as a testimony to the lost. Now the Israelites are encouraged by Samuel to turn away from their hypocritical lifestyle, professing to be God's people, but spending all of their time worshipping other things, and to become captors, not captives. Samuel knew that this radical spiritual revolution would not be easy. He challenged them to obey the directly stated will of God by putting away their false gods and then by joining him for some intense spiritual intercession. His prayer and their response turned the tide of circumstance.

The Lord thundered a great thunder as a result of their cries and the enemy was routed. At Samuel's direction Israel placed a rock to mark the victory and named it "Ebenezer," which means, "the Lord has helped us this far." In a similar way, God wants to not only place your Ebenezer, but to move it farther down the block today. There are people all around you who are wandering, void of God's presence and direction. You can, like Samuel, be encouraged that one person's prayers can make a difference. The question is, will you let Him? Will you allow Him to teach you to intercede in warfare for the welfare of yourself and others? If so, grab your combat boots and meet me at the window of prayer.

Winning back a rebellious heart

We read in the life of Hudson Taylor that during his rebellious teen years, his mother prayed this kind of intense prayer for him. Hudson's sister also joined her in prayers and fasting for his salvation. His mother, who was visiting friends at the time, excused herself from their company to turn aside and intercede for her son. She determined not to leave her "closet of prayer" until God gave her what she asked for. After quite some time in prayer she felt the peace of God about the matter. Miles away, Hudson was alone at home and bored. He picked up a tract left in his father's office and the Spirit of God impressed on him his need for salvation. He humbled his heart and received the Lord Jesus. Later when his mother came home he casually said, "I have something to tell you Mother." The one who had fought this spiritual war smiled and said simply, "I already know what it is." When God uses you in this kind of prayer you too will have the privilege of smiling, weary and battle scared, over the victories won in the closet, that later you see in reality.

A well-known speaker friend of mine, Rita Tate, tells of her rebellious teen years. One night she woke up with the sense that another person was in her room. Her godly mother was lying over the foot of her bed and interceding for her, the headstrong daughter who was going in the absolute wrong direction. She felt her heart soften as she listened to the pleading and the tears of her mother that night. Years later, after she had come to the Lord, she brought up the incident, never discussed before. "Momma, did I ever tell you that I heard you praying for me that night?" Her mother's answer was a surprise. "Honey, what do you mean THAT night? I prayed like that MANY nights over your bed."

"Usually prayer is a question of groaning rather than speaking, tears rather than words. For He sets our tears in His sight, and our groaning is not hidden from Him, who made all things by His Word and does not ask for words of man." Augustine of Hippo

My Uncle Kenny was a rough teenager. While some of the family members were shaking their heads over his rebelliousness towards God, my Grandma instead bowed her head in prayer. She wrestled in the invisible realm for forty years while some of us sat in disappointment watching this life being senselessly used up. Then at age forty Uncle Kenny gave his heart to the Lord. He started attending church and writing worship songs. Are there people in your life who are worth going to war over? It may take years of investment, but isn't one life worth every sacrifice?

"Work as if you were to live 100 years. Pray as if you were to die tomorrow." Benjamin Franklin

Prayer journal entry:

10/1/02 Prayed with Denise about a rebellious student in her Bible class.

1/15/03 Denise shared that this girl prayed to receive Christ and now has a softer attitude.

How to pray for a pre-Christian

There are many people that I am praying for who have not yet softened their hearts to the Lord. Over the years, I have compiled a list of verses that encourage me to keep on praying for them, and show me how to make my prayers effective for them. Perhaps it can be a helpful tool for you also. A word of caution, however, be careful when you come to the section on praying that circumstances will get their attention. After praying this consistently for a friend he almost lost his truck over the side of a mountain because his brakes gave out. A few weeks later he got trapped in his camper on a hot California day, with no one to hear his cries for help. He was rescued when out of the blue, his wife, strangely moved in thought, went to check on him. I am NOT encouraging you to pray harm into someone's life. I am saying that as a result of YOUR prayers God can pick out the kinds of circumstances that will get their attention and, if they respond, will save their souls from hell.

- **Pray that they will anticipate one moment past death, while there's still time to repent.**

"He is torn from the security of his tent, and they march him before the king of terrors." Job 18:14 "Complete darkness is held in reserve for his treasures, and unfanned fire will devour him; it will consume the survivor in his tent." Job 20:26 "For the wicked is reserved for the day of calamity; they will be led forth at the day of fury." Job 21:30 "Terrors overtake him like a flood; a tempest steals him away in the night." Job 27:20 "He will not escape from darkness; the flame will wither his shoots, and by the breath of His mouth he will go away." Job 15:30 "The wicked man writhes in pain all his days, and numbered are the years stored up for the ruthless. Sounds of terror are in his ears, while at peace the destroyer comes upon him. He does not believe that he will return from darkness, and he is destined for the sword. He wanders about for food, saying, 'Where is it?' He knows that a day of darkness is at hand. Distress and anguish terrify him, they overpower him like a king ready for the attack." Job 15:20-24

- **Pray for a breaking of pride/rebelliousness**

"Because he has stretched out his hand against God, and conducts himself arrogantly against the Almighty." Job 15:25 "O Lord, do not Thine eyes look for truth? Thou hast smitten them, but they did not weaken; Thou hast consumed them, but they refused to take correction. They have made their faces harder than rock; they have refused to repent." Jeremiah 5:3 "But this people has a stubborn and rebellious heart; they have turned aside and departed." Jeremiah 5:23 "Thus says the Lord, 'Stand by the ways and see and ask for the ancient paths, where the good way is, and walk in it; and you shall find rest for your souls.' But they said, 'We will not walk in it.' And I set watchmen over you, saying, 'Listen to the sound of the trumpet!' But they said, 'We will not listen.' Hear, O earth: behold, I am bringing disaster on this people, the fruit of their plans, because they have not listened to My words, and as for My law, they have rejected it also." Jeremiah 6:16-17, 19 "Yet they did not obey or incline their ear, but walked in their own counsels and in the stubbornness of their evil heart, and went backward and not forward. Yet they did not listen to Me or incline their ear, but stiffened their neck; they did evil more than their fathers." Jeremiah 7:24, 26 "Why then has this people, Jerusalem, turned away in continual apostasy? They hold fast to deceit, they refuse to return. I have listened and heard, they have spoken what is not right; no man repented of his wickedness, saying, 'What have I done?' Everyone turned to his course, like a horse charging into the battle." Jeremiah 8:5-6

- **Pray for a realization of the "emptiness" of what the world offers.**

"Thus says the Lord, 'What injustice did your fathers

find in Me, that they went far from Me and walked after emptiness and became empty?' " Jeremiah 2:5 "Let him not trust in emptiness, deceiving himself; for emptiness will be his reward." Job 15:31 "For the company of the godless is barren, and fire consumes the tents of the corrupt." Job 15:34 "For in many dreams and in many words there is emptiness. Rather, fear God." Ecclesiastes 5:7

- **Pray for God to speak to them through their dreams.**

"Indeed God speaks once, or twice, yet no one notices it. In a dream, a vision of the night, when sound sleep falls on men, while they slumber in their beds, then He opens the ears of men, and seals their instruction, that He may turn man aside from his conduct, and keep man from pride; He keeps back his soul from the pit, and his life from passing over into Sheol." Job 33:14-18

- **Pray for them to be able to see and hear truth.**

"To whom shall I speak and give warning, that they may hear? Behold, their ears are closed, and they cannot listen. Behold, the word of the Lord has become a reproach to them; they have no delight in it." Jeremiah 6:10 "'Behold, you are trusting in deceptive words to no avail. And now, because you have done all these things,' declares the Lord, 'and I spoke to you, rising up early and speaking, but you did not hear, and I called you but you did not answer.'" Jeremiah 7:8, 13 "You have seen many things, but you do not observe them; your ears are open, but none hears." Isaiah 42:20 "Because they did not obey the voice of the Lord their God, but transgressed His covenant, even all that Moses the servant of the Lord commanded; they would neither listen, nor do it." II Kings 18:12 "And He opens their *ear to instruction, and commands that they return from evil. If they hear and serve Him, they shall end their days in prosperity, and their years in pleasures. But if they do not hear, they shall perish by the sword, and they shall die without knowledge." Job 36:10-12*

- **Pray for him/her to see the "blessing of God" on His people and to desire it**

"Your iniquities have turned these away, and your sins have withheld good from you." Jeremiah 5:25 "Though he piles up silver like dust, and prepares garments as plentiful as the clay; he may prepare it, but the just will wear it, and the innocent will divide the silver." Job 27:16-17 "'I will surely snatch them away,' declares the Lord; 'There will be no grapes on the vine, and no figs on the fig tree, and the leaf shall wither; and what I have given them shall pass away.'" Jeremiah 8:13 "The increase of his house will depart; his possessions will flow away in the day of his anger. This is the wicked man's portion from God, even the heritage decreed to him by God." Job 20:28-29 "The One forming light and creating darkness, causing well-being and creating calamity; I am the Lord who does all these." Isaiah 45:7 "For by me your days will be multiplied, and years of life will be added to you." Proverbs 9:11

- **Pray for the conviction of conscience and shame of sin.**

"Were they ashamed because of the abomination they had done? They certainly were not ashamed, and they did not know how to blush; therefore they shall fall among those who fall; at the time of their punishment they shall be brought down,' declares the Lord." Jeremiah 8:12 "Let us lie down in our shame, and let our humiliation cover us; for

we have sinned against the Lord our God, we and our fathers, since our youth even to this day. And we have not obeyed the voice of the Lord our God." Jeremiah 3:25 "Transgression speaks to the ungodly within his heart; there is no fear of God before his eyes." Psalm 36:1

- **Pray that the secrets of the heart would be revealed through God's people.**

"The secrets of his heart are disclosed; and so he will fall on his face and worship God, declaring that God is certainly among you." I Corinthians 14:25

- **Pray that he/she will tire of the deception of Satan.**

"'And they bend their tongue like their bow; lies and not truth prevail in the land; for they proceed from evil to evil, and they do not know Me,' declares the Lord. 'Let everyone be on guard against his neighbor, and do not trust any brother; because every brother deals craftily, and every neighbor goes about as a slanderer. And everyone deceives his neighbor, and does not speak the truth, they have taught their tongue to speak lies; they weary themselves committing iniquity. Your dwelling is in the midst of deceit; through deceit they refuse to know Me,' declares the Lord. Therefore thus says the Lord of hosts, 'Behold, I will refine them and assay them; for what else can I do, because of the daughter of My people?'" Jeremiah 9:3-7 "You are of your father the devil, and you want to do the desires of your father. He was a murderer from the beginning, and does not stand in the truth, because there is no truth in him. Whenever he speaks a lie, he speaks from his own nature; for he is a liar, and the father of lies." John 8:44 "And everyone deceives his neighbor, and does not speak the truth, they have taught their tongue to speak lies; they weary themselves committing iniquity." Jeremiah 9:5

- **Pray for them to seek God's unlimited compassion.**

   "If you would seek God and implore the compassion of the Almighty, if you are pure and upright, surely now He would rouse Himself for you and restore your righteous estate." Job 8:5-6 "And nothing from that which is put under the ban shall cling to your hand, in order that the Lord may turn from His burning anger and show mercy to you, and have compassion on you and make you increase, just as He has sworn to your fathers." Deuteronomy 13:17 "But God, being rich in mercy, because of His great love with which He loved us, even when we were dead in our transgressions, made us alive together with Christ (by grace you have been saved), and raised us up with Him, and seated us with Him in the heavenly places, in Christ Jesus, in order that in the ages to come He might show the surpassing riches of His grace in kindness toward us in Christ Jesus." Ephesians 2:4-7

- **Pray for the witness of the Creator through creation.**

   "The heavens are telling of the glory of God; and their expanse is declaring the work of His hands. Day to day pours forth speech, and night to night reveals knowledge. There is no speech, nor are there words; their voice is not heard." Psalm 19:1-3 "Because that which is known about God is evident within them; for God made it evident to them. For since the creation of the world His invisible attributes, His eternal power and divine nature, have been clearly seen, being understood through what has been made, so that they are without excuse." Romans 1:19-20 "'Do you not fear Me?' declares the Lord. 'Do you not tremble in My presence? For I have placed the sand as a boundary for the sea, an eternal decree, so it cannot cross over it. Though the waves toss, yet they cannot prevail; though they roar, yet they cannot cross over it.'" Jeremiah

5:22 *"When I consider Thy heavens, the work of Thy fingers, the moon and the stars, which Thou hast ordained; what is man, that Thou dost take thought of him? And the son of man, that Thou dost care for him?" Psalm 8:3-4 "By the word of the Lord the heavens were made, and by the breath of His mouth all their host. He gathers the waters of the sea together as a heap; He lays up the deeps in storehouses. Let all the earth fear the Lord; let all the inhabitants of the world stand in awe of Him. For He spoke, and it was done; He commanded, and it stood fast." Psalm 33:6-9 "O Lord, our Lord, how majestic is Thy name in all the earth, who hast displayed Thy splendor above the heavens!" Psalm 8:1*

- **Pray that God will use whatever circumstances necessary to get their attention.**

"'Who is the wise man that may understand this? And who is he to whom the mouth of the Lord has spoken that he may declare it? Why is the land ruined, laid waste like a desert, so that no one passes through?' And the Lord said, 'Because they have forsaken My law which I set before them, and have not obeyed My voice nor walked according to it.'" Jeremiah 9:12-13 "Then I will make to cease from the cities of Judah and from the streets of Jerusalem the voice of joy and the voice of gladness, the voice of the bridegroom and the voice of the bride; for the land will become a ruin." Jeremiah 7:34 "Because they do not regard the works of the Lord nor the deeds of His hands, He will tear them down and not build them up." Psalm 28:5

- **Pray for them to experience their need for God's wisdom in daily decision making.**

"And they say to God, 'Depart from us! We do not even

desire the knowledge of Thy ways.'" Job 21:14 *"The wise men are put to shame, they are dismayed and caught; behold, they have rejected the word of the Lord, and what kind of wisdom do they have?"* Jeremiah 8:9 *"Counsel is mine and sound wisdom; I am understanding, power is mine."* Proverbs 8:14 *"For the Lord gives wisdom; from His mouth come knowledge and understanding."* Proverbs 2:6 *"A scoffer seeks wisdom, and finds none, but knowledge is easy to him who has understanding."* Proverbs 14:6 *"For wisdom is protection just as money is protection. But the advantage of knowledge is that wisdom preserves the lives of its possessors."* Ecclesiastes 7:12 *"And to man He said, 'Behold, the fear of the Lord, that is wisdom; and to depart from evil is understanding.'"* Job 28:28

"Intercession is the most unselfish thing anyone can do." Paul Billheimer, <u>Destined for the Throne</u> p. 107.

3

Witnessing God's Projects

Sometimes the Lord asks us to do something that requires us to be sustained by resources we cannot yet see, such as when the work of God outgrows a facility. This has happened several times in the history of our church. There was a period of time, before we could see the next level of resource, when we had to make commitments for expansion.

In December of 1991, we felt the Lord leading us to seek a more permanent facility that would not have to be set up each week. (Up to this point we had rented school facilities.) We looked at several buildings, but none were really within our resources. My husband felt that we should rent space in an available industrial building, but with weekly offerings of about five hundred dollars, the two thousand dollars a month lease payment looked IMPOSSIBLE. We would have to complete the renovating project (removing roll up doors, replacing them with walls, hanging fire doors, etc.) in twenty-one days in order to avoid double payments (which the church could not afford). Knowing what we know now about build-outs, plan checks, and inspections, we might not have even attempted such a feat in such a limited time period. However, God was with us. Though we received the final sign off at 7pm on the last Friday evening there was still much to do before our first worship service. The building had to be painted. This was done through the night by a small crew of people-mostly teens. Carpet was laid on Saturday, and we worshipped in awe that Sunday morning. We witnessed God doing the IMPOSSIBLE.

It was here in this building that we began to feel God call us to begin our preschool and elementary school. Both were begun with zero church funds, mega faith and sincere obedience. Many times we saw the impossible accomplished as fire inspections were passed, equipment was donated and staff was secured. One of the greatest miracles we witnessed was when we finally acquired the eleven hundred square feet of playground space, in conformity with local codes, so that we could start our preschool. We had seen the pieces falling into place in regards to the preschool, but this was one obstacle we couldn't seem to conquer. We had looked into renting adjacent properties, using existing grassy areas and inside play space all with no green lights. I remember sitting in our car, waiting for my husband to join me after the morning worship service. As I sat, I prayed "God, You know that this is Your work. Why can't you just show us how it can be done?" As I looked up from my prayer I noticed something I had never seen before. Straight-ahead between our sanctuary and the next business was a small area of bushes. Suddenly the thought came, "I wonder how much square footage there is on this little patch of land?" When my husband came out, I urged him to go get his measuring tape. Sure enough, this little piece of property was forty more sq. feet than we needed to meet the regulation. Again, we had seen God conform our plans to His will.

As our schools grew, our landlord began to smile less and less. We all knew that we needed to look elsewhere for enough space for the growing number of children. The owner made the decision easier by raising the rent and tightening up the space that we could use. All during this time, we were looking at every facility and any open land that was available. Of course, we were also praying steadily. One day we were told that our school would have to move by the next fall. Where do you move an existing school? We knew that endless codes require specifications that are difficult to meet. As I talked with Ms. McD____, who was our administrator at that time, I encouraged her with these words: "I don't know how God is going to do it, but I know He has a way. This school was called into existence by His power, and He will sustain us through this faith journey." I saw the discouragement in her face turn to hope, and she began calling local churches to see if any of them had space available. In one day she found a beautiful facility in our area that NEEDED help with their expenses to continue their ministry. The Lord had answered their prayers and ours.

God used this inconvenient move to a new school facility to begin unifying the pastors of our city. Three of them now shared the same facilities for a portion of every week. God had prompted our hearts to begin praying for revival every Saturday evening. We initially met in our home, and then eventually moved to Corona's Civic Center. God worked to develop a bond of friendship between the pastors who prayed with us and we saw that He often used this method of sharing facilities to accomplish His purposes. God was using "facility crises situations" to build His church. God began moving in the ministerial meetings causing a strong bond to develop among the pastors in attendance and breaking down the barriers that kept us from working together. Many pastors began coming that had formerly minimized the importance of this time of sharing.

When God says "Go," but circumstances say "No."

"Now the sons of the prophets said to Elisha, 'Behold now, the place before you where we are living is too limited for us. Please let us go to the Jordan, and each of us take from there a beam, and let us make a place there for ourselves where we may live.' So he said, 'Go.' Then one said, 'Please be willing to go with your servants.' And he answered, 'I shall go.' So he went with them; and when they came to the Jordan, they cut down trees. But as one was felling a beam, the ax head fell into the water; and he cried out and said, 'Alas, my master! For it was borrowed.' Then the man of God said, 'Where did it fall?' And when he showed him the place, he cut off a stick, and threw it in there, and made the iron float. And he said, 'Take it up for yourself.' So he put out his hand and took it." II Kings 6:1-7

According to this passage, when the sons of the prophets proposed an expansion plan, God responded through His prophet Elisha, "Go!" The prophets, however, may have found the word "go" perplexing. The day after God said "go" they were not yet able to see the provision of God for the work. (They couldn't even afford their own ax!) But the work began simply because the prophets asked, "Should we go?" and God said, "Go!" This has been God's pattern from the beginning. For example, He said, "Let there be light," and it was so. The WORD of God spoke everything in creation into existence. God said, "Abraham, you will have a son and through him all the families of the world will be blessed." And it was done. We need to learn to trust God at moment of His command, not later, at the moment of supply.

In March of 2002, as I was praying, the Lord spoke to my heart about the need for our church to begin a junior high school. When I told God all the reasons why this wasn't possible He gave me a very stern reply, which I took to heart.

"Who are you to tell me what I can and cannot do?" I continued praying about this request and as I was praying, I specifically saw our Educational Administrator's face in connection with this project. When I mentioned it to him a few days later he informed me that he wasn't even sure he would be staying at our school for the coming year because of financial needs. "He doesn't seem to have been informed about your plan Lord," I thought. Then, about a week later, I learned that additional salary had been provided and that he would be staying with our school. I took these circumstances over which I had no control and their direct CHANGE as confirmation to believe God will help us to one day have a junior high.

Take up the beam of prayer

The building materials God uses for His work are spiritual. Therefore to assist God in His work requires moving up to the heavenly realm where resources are authorized and plans are finalized for our earthly existence. Here's another passage of Scripture to encourage us in the construction process of God's projects.

In Daniel 10:12 we see that an answer to Daniel's prayer was authorized immediately. *"Then he said to me, 'Do not be afraid, Daniel, for from the first day that you set your heart on understanding this and on humbling yourself before your God, your words were heard, and I have come in response to your words.'"* However, it was 21 days until Daniel saw with human eyes the answer to his prayer. *"In those days I, Daniel, had been mourning for three entire weeks. I did not eat any tasty food, nor did meat or wine enter my mouth, nor did I use any ointment at all, until the entire three weeks were completed. And on the twenty-fourth day of the first month, while I was by the bank of the great river, that is, the Tigris, I lifted my eyes and looked, and behold, there was a certain man dressed in linen, whose waist was girded with a belt of pure gold of Uphaz." Daniel 10:2-5*

From the above passage, we see that there are two realms in which we operate when we are praying. There is the spirit realm, which is where resources are dispatched and warfare is waged. There is also the physical realm, which is where we finally see the outcome of our praying. It's kind of like going to a drive-through restaurant. One window is where you order and one window is where you finally get your food. Depending on the restaurant and what you've ordered there is a waiting time period between the two windows. You don't know how long the wait will be. In the same way, some things are accomplished in the spirit realm long before we see their reality in our lives.

For example, we see this truth illustrated in Daniel chapter 10. Daniel notices something through his reading of the Word of God. He notices the number of weeks that Israel will be in captivity and realizes they are nearing completion. Therefore he turns his attention to seek the face of God, to acknowledge his sin, and the sin of his people, and to humbly offer repentance. In response, God dispatches an angel, who is to equip Daniel with understanding for this particular time. When the angel appears, we see that he has been fasting for three weeks. The angel points out that when Daniel FIRST began to pray about this matter, he was sent out, but that he was waging spiritual warfare for twenty-one days against the "Prince of Persia."

So for twenty-one days Daniel had an answer to his prayers in the heavenly realm, but he did not experience the blessing until twenty-one days later. This has happened to me on occasion when my prayer was not answered right away, and I believe that it is an important lesson to understand in order to walk in victory amid perplexing circumstances and delays.

For example, in 2002 we began praying for the money to build a playground for our school. A few fund-raisers were put in motion and we began to seek the favor of the Lord. One day, in September of 2002, I was praying about this very matter, when the Lord prompted me to read Is. 65:24: *"It will also come to pass that before they call, I will answer; and while they are still speaking, I will hear."* God has a way of highlighting His Word in our hearts when it is both general AND personal. Consequently, I knew at that time that we had the request we had asked of the Lord. However, it wasn't until December 13th that we could give a praise report: we could order our new playground equipment! During that waiting period, when the answer to our request looked unlikely, the Lord wanted us to have something to hold on to. Like a parent giving a baby his pacifier, He gave us this verse to calm our hearts when our next "meal" looked too far away.

Prayer journal entry:

8/25/02 Received phone call from a friend, Rita. She has been disturbed by a dream in which our mutual friend Kris is crying. She believes someone in the dream has died. The dream leaves her tremendously burdened. She has interceded, but wants me to join her in this effort. (I have known Rita for years and am convinced of her spiritual maturity. She has never been associated with gossip. She is a true intercessor. I take this information to heart and begin praying for comfort for what we cannot see in Kris' life.)

9/1/02 Kris calls in the middle of the night. Her father, who has been undergoing some health difficulties, has been rushed to the hospital. The doctors are not sure he will make it through the night. We pray that Kris will be able to pray with him to make sure he's ready to meet the Lord. She is not sure where her mom stands with the Lord either.

Because her sister is a Mormon, Kris is afraid that her mom might interfere with the process for the sake of family peace. We pray that if she should leave, that it would be to use the restroom. She ends up staying and listening to the entire conversation. Kris' dad assures his daughter that he is ready to meet the Lord and this brings great comfort to her. In my mind I thought this encounter was why God had prompted Rita to pray for her.

10/3/02 Kris finds her mother dead in her home on this morning. She is found in a kneeling position. The Coroner determines that she died the evening before as she was getting ready for bed. Two things comfort Kris: When she was little her mother always had her kneel to say her bedtime prayers. Also, a picture of Jesus is found in her mother's wallet with the saying, "He's my friend." These two indications give Kris the comfort that her mother was praying and that her heart was right with God before her death. Isn't God good to have tapped one of His servants to war for Kris at a time when comfort was such an essential commodity?

In 2001 I was attending a service where God's spirit was tender and heavy. We were hushed in powerful worship when out of the blue I saw a friend's face shining with the love of the Lord. What made this so remarkable was that this man is not a believer yet. (He has slowly been making his way from atheism to agnosticism to the yard next to salvation's fence.) I had simply been worshipping and the Lord responded by sharing one of His intimate secrets for the future. I now know that some day this man will hop over that fence and give his heart to the Lord. I may have to wait a while between the window of asking and the window of getting, but it's going to happen. This helps his wife and me as we pray. We pray differently as a result.

"And he said to his servant, 'Go up now, look toward the

sea.' So he went up and looked and said, 'There is nothing.' And he said, 'Go back' seven times. And it came about at the seventh time, that he said, 'Behold, a cloud as small as a man's hand is coming up from the sea.' And he said, 'Go up, say to Ahab, Prepare your chariot and go down, so that the heavy shower does not stop you.' So it came about in a little while, that the sky grew black with clouds and wind, and there was a heavy shower. And Ahab rode and went to Jezreel." I Kings 18:43-45

In the account of Elijah on Mt. Carmel we see another incident of this truth lived out. God has told Elijah, who has been avoiding King Ahab, to show his face to the king. God has already told Elijah that Israel will have no rain until King Ahab sees him again, so putting the pieces together, Elijah KNOWS that today it is going to rain. However, checking the weather report or sending a servant to have a look outside turns up the same disappointing results: Elijah is told that "there is nothing." There is no rain. There is not even a cloud in the sky. We then see a reflection of Elijah's tenacity in prayer as he sends his servant back six more times! A tenacity, which is born out of God's repeated confirmation that He will do what He says, even though Elijah cannot yet see the confirmation in the physical realm. Finally on the seventh trip the servant sees a little cloud. This is all Elijah needs to know. They grab the umbrellas and hit the road because Elijah knows what kind of storm was coming. (It was going to be the kind that would represent God's heart of grace, love and forgiveness to a repentant nation.)

Don't give up

One of the most difficult prayer lessons to learn is to keep praying even when you don't see any progress being made by your prayers. Many times we give up too soon in our asking. We weary of waiting at the window.

In August of 2002 a close friend, in our church, told us that he felt the Lord wanted him and my husband to travel to Uganda for a special week of meetings at an orphanage our church helped sponsor. My husband was not sure what this was all about, but he presented it to the elders of our church and they agreed that if the Lord provided the funds for this trip, that it would confirm that they should go.

I remember making a little chart to help raise funds for the trip. I used little airplanes to each represent fifty dollars in funds raised. There sure were a lot of little airplanes! There were more fifty dollar increments than I thought were possible for our church at that time. As I was putting this chart together the Lord laid this passage of scripture on me: *"He says, 'It is too small a thing that you should be my servant to raise up the tribes of Jacob, and to restore the preserved ones of Israel; I will also make you a light of the nations so that My salvation may reach to the end of the earth.'" (Isaiah 49:6)* I know that this passage was initially written as a prophecy of Christ saving the world, but at that moment it was as if God stuck that verse, like a Post-it-note, on my forehead. God was making a point: this job was a small thing for Him. He was going to do something even BIGGER than provide for this trip: He was going to use us to reach the nations. I sat down in wonder at the thought.

As September came and went, only about five hundred dollars had come in for the trip. October crept by with hardly any action at all, but in my quiet time each day the Lord's leading through Scripture made my faith grow. It was as if I could touch and taste the trip in my prayer time. However in the physical realm **there was nothing**. In November I mentioned to Wayne, the other traveler, that he'd better get his passport, that in my quiet times God had been confirming that they WOULD be going.

In December, the favorable impressions continued. Since

the trip was scheduled for early January, I began asking my husband if he had gotten his shots. He couldn't understand why he should. The money hadn't come in, he reasoned. I felt that an act of faith was necessary on his part. How could he take no step of faith and expect the "Jordan waters" to dry up around his feet? The next day (Wednesday) without telling me, he got his shots. The following day, I had an extraordinary quiet time. When I prayed about the trip I experienced something difficult to talk about. In the middle of the request for this trip the Lord spoke clearly to my heart and said "It's done, don't ask me about it again." Elated and amazed I ended my prayer time and wondered what to do next. Should I email friends and family to ask for money? No, God had said the job was done. I felt that my hands were tied to do anything but trust Him, but that was hard to do.

A year or so before this time we had had a woman in our church who occasionally gave out a "prophetic word" to someone. When the elders became aware that many of these "words" had not come true, they felt they must follow the Biblical mandate and ask her to either admit her error or leave the church. She chose to leave the church. This thought circled my head as I fought to believe God's Word to me for that moment in time. "If I'm wrong, it's going to be a difficult for my husband when they have to ask me to leave," I thought. (Smile.)

I E-mailed Wayne and told him that the Lord had definitely confirmed that they were going. He surprised me when he answered that he had not gotten his passport or shots. He had already taken time off from work to spend time with relatives (the missionaries who operated the orphanage in Uganda) because it seemed nothing was happening with the money for the trip.

I got off the computer and dialed my prayer partner. Weeping, I told her that I didn't understand what was happening. How could I feel such a confirmation from the Lord and yet be faced with such an impossible situation? We prayed together and my heart was comforted. All day long I was in the spirit of prayer for this trip.

In the evening my daughter was to take a gymnastic lesson and since I had left the check for her lessons at home, I asked my husband if he would run home and bring it to us after work that day. When he came to the gym, he said he had something VERY important to tell me. That very day a huge gift that was specified for missions had been received! It easily covered the entire trip (and several others that have been taken since that time.) I thought I would explode in praise!

That night my husband and I met with the other couple for prayer. Certainly the funds had come in, but there were many more details that looked just as impossible: Wayne didn't have his passport or shots, neither man had a stamped visa from Washington. Wayne needed time off from work and we didn't have any airline reservations. This was ten days from when the trip was supposed to begin.

On Friday, Wayne, who had the day off, drove down to the passport office in Los Angeles. Anyone who has ever tried to get a passport quickly knows what an ordeal it is, and that it normally takes at least six weeks. He didn't have the exact documentation they needed, so he had to drive back to Riverside to get it and then return to Los Angeles before they closed that evening. They took his paperwork and assured him that if his wife could drive back down on Monday the passport would be issued and ready.

Late Friday evening I began looking on the Internet for ticket prices. A typical fare to Uganda could cost from two to three thousand dollars, and it wasn't until around midnight that I found two round-trip fares and a night's hotel in London for the bargain price of two thousand six hundred and fifty dollars. By then, everyone, including my husband was asleep. I was in a quandary because it seemed like a great price, but I am not a good person for details. I didn't want to make a mistake with that amount of money, even though it seemed too good to pass up. I prayed, got my husband's OK and then ordered the tickets. The next morning when I returned to the site to get airport directions and such, I noticed that you could no longer buy tickets for that flight. It was now completely booked.

That Saturday, our family was planning to enjoy a day at an amusement park as the guests of a friend, but someone had to wait outside for family members who had gotten lost in traffic. I volunteered because it gave me more time to pray about the trip. I wasn't sure at this point if I had done the right thing in ordering the tickets and was pleading with the Lord for His help. When I got home there was a message on the answering machine from our coordinating missionary. He said, "I hope you didn't already buy those tickets. I think you can do better than that price." My heart sank as I heard his words and dialed his number. As it turned out he thought I had paid two thousand six hundred and fifty for **each** ticket, not the two combined. The Lord had made it all work out right.

On Monday, Wayne's wife Kathy, picked up his passport as promised and put it with my husbands' in an envelope addressed to the Ugandan Embassy in Washington. This process of stamping passports can take several weeks, but because God's hand was in it, a woman in the office opened the envelope, stamped them and overnighted them back to us. We had them in our hands two days later. Wayne got his shots on Wednesday, the suitcases were packed with love, prayer and gifts for the children in the orphanage and the two men left on Sunday for their adventure. What an amazing God we have!

We also know, from Abraham's life, that faith is the other crucial building material God uses to fulfill His purposes. God didn't use Abraham because He was smart, capable, organized or thrifty. God completed an impossible work through him because he BELIEVED. This was Elisha's mode when he commanded the ax head to come up out of the water. He was walking in full assurance of God's authority over the situation. If God says, "Go," then circumstances must obey also.

"Prayer puts one in touch with a planet. I can as really be touching hearts for God in far away India or China through prayer as though I were there." "A man may go aside today, and shut his door, and as really spend a half hour in India for God... as though he were there in person." S.D. Gordon, <u>Quiet Talks on Prayer.</u>

Has God commissioned this project?

An important question to ask in the beginning of all projects is "Whose project is it?" It is so easy for our egos and ambitions to take the place of pure devotion and passion. The beginning of our elementary school, which was one of the greatest adventures of my life, took place in January of 1999 with a casual quiet time. I had been evaluating schools in the area because my daughter Beth would be starting kindergarten in the fall. I had visited a local Christian school (too expensive) and a special magnet school and our local neighborhood school. I had been totally discouraged by these visits. For admission at the public schools, my five-year-old daughter would have had to sign an agreement that she would not carry a knife, gun, or *sell* drugs. Maybe this doesn't blow the rest of you away, but I was expecting something like "I promise not to chew gum, say bad words or hit." The reality of where our world had come to was present in my thoughts, but it was not the agenda of my quiet time. I felt God speak to my heart these words: "Why don't you start a school?" Immediately there were a hundred responses. "We don't have money, we don't have equipment, I am not capable or qualified…" You get the idea. But I knew God had spoken.

As I worked through Henry Blackaby's, **Experiencing God** workbook, I was touched by the fact that when God spoke to someone in the Old Testament: (p.20) they always knew it was God. They knew what God was saying. They also knew what they were to do in response. In the same way I can tell you that I knew what God was asking us to do.

I proceeded by presenting the idea to our leadership board at church. Unfortunately, God had not given them a *heads up* on His plan. The idea of starting a school came out of the blue for them. They had not had the experience of hearing Him speak up to that point. Some were excited, many were cautious and a few people thought the idea was down-right ridiculous. This group of people had seen God do some pretty amazing things, so they agreed to pray about it during the coming month and return to the discussion then.

The next month we agreed to put out a fleece, similar to what Gideon had done centuries ago. We decided if we had eight students by Aug. 1st that our school could open. If you think this was a simple endeavor, review with me the incredible elements laid out for the Lord to accomplish. If He wanted the school to open He would have to provide everything the school would need: students, teacher, books and equipment in just a few short months and all with no budget.

Every morning I would begin with the Word of God and prayer. "If I have gotten this all mixed up, God, and this isn't you, would you please show me?" was how most mornings began. Then I would read the Word and God's part of the conversation would take place. I got to hear His heart for the lives of children. I got reminded of how He loves it when we trust Him to do the impossible and I would find my heart being carried away with HOPE.

Then my quiet time would end and I would face the million and one tasks on my "to do" list, a barren checkbook and a lot of people asking me *how* it was going to get done. One by one students would come in to check out our "school." There wasn't much besides my faith to show them on the tour, but by June we had six students. I had to go on vacation, but I didn't want to. I wanted to stay and work at getting the final students registered. God had a different plan. He wanted to make sure that I was going to "be still and find out once again that He was God."

We had chosen to spend some time with my parents in Pasadena and while my Dad (another pastor) was at a board meeting I had to get an *I-V* for my shaky faith from God's Word. "Was this God's will? Had I heard correctly?" Many people's lives were going to be affected by the accuracy of my spiritual hearing. I read through the entire New Testament that night marking the verses that were God's post it notes for me. When I finished, I knew again that He had pressed His heart on mine. You can read these faith-inspiring verses at *www.oliveleafpublications.com* if you are interested.

One thought, that encouraged me on this journey, was the result of some research that I had done for a video on Free Methodist (FM) schools. Before I married my Southern Baptist husband, I had grown up in the FM church. One thing that had impressed me about the (FM) Light and Life Schools in California was that people just like us had started each one. They had limited educational backgrounds, no financial backing, and little justification to take on the project (extra space lying around their churches, lots of free time on their hands, etc.) I also remember reading about how Yale University began. Ten pastors made the commitment to start the school and even gave up their own books for the library. Classes met in one pastor's home. They simply shared a desire to see ministers trained.

One particular passage that ministered to my heart during this crucial period of waiting was *"In hope against hope he believed, in order that he might become a father of many nations, according to that which had been spoken, 'So shall your descendants be.' And without becoming weak in faith he contemplated his own body, now as good as dead since he was about a hundred years old, and the deadness of Sarah's womb; yet, with respect to the promise of God, he did not waver in unbelief, but grew strong in faith, giving glory to God." Romans 4:1-20*

On Aug. 1st, I sat waiting for what we needed: one more student to enroll. As the day went by and no new students came in to register I began to be frustrated. "God, You know that every single day I have come before you and asked You to direct me. All along the way I have given You every opportunity to correct me if I'm wrong. You have only encouraged me by Your Word. You have sent people, resources and fueled the fire. You can't leave us now. You can't cause people to laugh and say, "You're not powerful enough to do this thing."

There was a thought that came after my prayer time. "If there are no new students coming in today, maybe there is someone who ALREADY came through the doors who couldn't enroll for one reason or another." I began looking through the files and sure enough, there had been one student who wanted to attend, but didn't have enough money. Two people had told me, along this journey, that if there was ANYTHING they could do to make the project GO, I should ask. I called the mother to see if her son still wanted to attend and to find out what they could afford. They wanted him to come to our school in a big way, but could only afford about half the tuition. We were then able to contact the TWO people, who were more than willing to cover a fourth of the tuition via a scholarship, and by seven PM that night we had our eight students.

Now, as I see the many, many children running around

our school, I remember that it is our God who "calls things into existence," and I will never be tricked into thinking that human hands started our school. So when your prayer request looks as good as dead and you see NOTHING, do what Elijah did and do what we did: **Go back**. Head into your prayer closet and keep your umbrella nearby. Keep in mind that God Himself says in His Word: *Let none that wait on Thee be ashamed.*

"It proves afresh, that, if our work is His work, and we honor Him, by waiting upon and looking to Him for means, He will surely, in His own time and way, supply them." George Mueller, Answers to Prayer, *p. 65*

Prayer journal entry:

7/14/01 God told me to prepare a chapel for our school children on the development of a child in the womb to combat the "worldview" of abortion.

2/15/02 The chapel was given. God gave the points for a PowerPoint presentation, the idea for a craft and an original song to make it memorable.

"And I searched for a man among them who should build up the wall and stand in the gap before Me for the land, that I should not destroy it; but I found no one." Ezekiel 22:30

Some times people get confused about God's message. If they are not in the Word, they might announce that God approves of homosexuality. If they are lax about being in His presence they might say that God approves of a Christian couple living together before marriage. But if we are saturating ourselves in God's Word and if we are faithful to stand in His presence, **we will know His heart and be**

able to determine His will. These two, along with the ever present Holy Spirit's prompting act like checks and balances in the decision-making process. God says His sheep know His voice. If this is the right direction, we will hear a voice that tells us, *"this is the way." (John 10:27) "And your ears will hear a word behind you, 'This is the way, walk in it,' whenever you turn to the right or to the left." (Isaiah 30:21) "You shall follow the Lord your God and fear Him; and you shall keep His commandments, listen to His voice, serve Him, and cling to Him. (Deuteronomy 13:4) "But this is what I commanded them, saying, 'Obey My voice, and I will be your God, and you will be My people; and you will walk in all the way which I command you, that it may be well with you.'" (Jeremiah 7:23)*

So how do we determine if the voice we hear is that of the Lord or not? Ann Graham-Lotz has a wonderful message on this very subject. (This message is found on the tape series from her ***Just Give Me Jesus*** seminar.) It's based on the parable of the sheepfold. She opens up our understanding of John 10:1-5 by describing the winter sheepfold used in Jesus' day. All the shepherds would bring their sheep to one fold, which was protected by high walls. One shepherd would remain through the night with all the sheep and in the morning would open the door from the inside as he recognized the voice of the true shepherds. They would then each wait outside and call their respective sheep one by one by name. As the sheep heard their shepherd call the familiar sound of their name, they would go outside.

"Truly, truly, I say to you, he who does not enter by the door into the fold of the sheep, but climbs up some other way, he is a thief and a robber. But he who enters by the door is a shepherd of the sheep. ***To him the doorkeeper opens****, and the sheep hear his voice, and he calls his own sheep by name, and leads them out. When he puts forth all his own,*

he goes before them, and the sheep follow him because they know his voice. And a stranger they simply will not follow, but will flee from him, because they do not know the voice of strangers." John 10:1-5

Ann teaches that the door of the sheepfold is God's Word. There is no way to hear Him speak without crossing its threshold. She describes the doorkeeper as the Holy Spirit, who recognizes the voice of God and opens our hearts to hear His instructions. The Holy Spirit is like the tilt device on a pinball machine. Stray from the truth and you hear warning bells go off. Many times what people think they are hearing from God is totally opposed to His Word and His Will. Warning bells go off in the hearts of those who know the true shepherd. So the best way to be accurate in our hearing is to stay close to His Word and His heart.

When the voice we hear lines up with God's Word and heart, each of us is to "take up a beam" in the building process. We are to take up the responsibility of seeking the Lord, like Daniel, until His perfect will is accomplished. Like the people in Nehemiah's time, we may not be able to build the entire wall, but we can exercise the faith needed to fix the front of our own house. We can each be responsible to earnestly press God for the fulfillment of His will. To carry a beam is not easy work. To carry the burden of God will be equally demanding.

The expansion will not be without hindrances. God said, "Go!" and they did, but that didn't mean they would not experience days when the ax head was at the bottom of the Jordan River. God wants us all to "get" the idea of using hindrances as opportunities. If the sons of the prophets had not faced the prospect of no progress (an ax head under water) and seen it defeated, their faith would have remained puny and ineffective.

The hindrances are NOT to stop the work. The ax head

falling in the river was never meant by God to stop the work, but to increase it. Do you think those young prophets ministered differently because they witnessed the God of the impossible bringing an ax head out of the water? Of course they did. And God wants to take each of us from the place where we are learning (like the sons of the prophets) to the place of doing (bringing the ax head up out of the water with a confident faith, like Elisha). But we will have to face days where the work comes to a stand still before His righteous indignation rises up inside us and we remind an ax head, a person, or the government that God said "GO!"

God's approval of an expansion project does not imply that we will never temporarily experience a *need*. (They had to borrow an ax.) But we should live expecting God to meet every NEED once it has been recognized. (An ax was lent to them at the time they *needed* one.) We are not to be content in a true state of NEED. We are to look longingly at our Lord who has promised to meet every NEED. We are to meet Him at His chambers every day, knocking and pleading until our reality matches what He has promised in His Word. It is His job to sort out our wants from our needs. We don't have enough brainpower for that job. What appears to be *a need* might just be *a want* in disguise. But real needs become obvious with time. When you borrowed an ax and you are responsible to return it, and you don't have the resources to replace it, that's a need. Especially when you are doing the work that God sent you to do in the first place.

God wanted to use a borrowed ax so that not only would the sons of the prophets see a miracle, but other people, like the one who lent the ax, would have the benefit of witnessing God's miraculous work. Many times we wonder why God allows the world to see our needs. It is so that THEY will know that He is God when the needs have been faithfully met.

When our school has a need, and God meets it, all the families and their relatives become aware of God's provision.

If we are trying to BE God instead of just worshipping Him, we will try to fill all the needs ourselves (we will quickly discover it to be an impossible job) and rob the world of the greatest show on earth, the intervention of the true, the powerful, living God. Our school administrator and I had a conversation about this very thing. She said that she tried to "protect" the teachers from the knowledge of a financial need. I urged her to let them share God's roller coaster adventure ride. There is no way we can control its twists and turns. We simply buckle ourselves in with His all-powerful trustworthy seat belt and enjoy the ride.

Prayer journal entry:

1/3/02 We agreed with the prayer of the second graders at Olive Branch Christian Academy. They are squished into a small classroom in our new building because county regulations say they must be on the ground floor. We have a county agent coming out to reconsider the rule in light of our particular circumstances. (If they were able to move upstairs they would have a huge classroom and their own fire exit for safety. It looks reasonable to us, but then we're not the county.)

1/7/02 We are given permission to move the second grade class upstairs. Twenty little children have now seen that God can solve their problems.

Here are some verses to encourage you to engage the enemy for the return of lives, resources and opportunity – *"Now I urge you, brethren, by our Lord Jesus Christ and by the love of the Spirit **to strive together with me** in your prayers to God for me." Romans 15:30 "Finally, brethren, **pray for us that the word of the Lord may spread rapidly and be glorified**, just as it did also with you." I Thessalonians 3:1 "As we **night and day keep praying most***

earnestly *that we may see your face, and may complete what is lacking in your faith?" 1Thessalonians 3: 10-11 "I thank God, whom I serve with a clear conscience the way my forefathers did, as I constantly remember you in my prayers* **night and day.***" Timothy 1:3 "Rejoicing in hope, persevering in tribulation,* **devoted** *to prayer." Romans 12:12 "For God, whom I serve in my spirit in the preaching of the gospel of His Son, is my witness as to how* **unceasingly I make mention of you,** *always in my prayers making request, if perhaps now at last by the will of God I may succeed in coming to you." Romans 1:9-10 "He trains my hands for battle,* **so that my arms can bend a bow of bronze.***" Psalm 18:34 "I will go before you and make the rough places smooth; I will shatter the doors of bronze, and cut through their iron bars.* **And I will give you the treasures of darkness, and hidden wealth of secret places,** *in order that you may know that it is I, The Lord, the God of Israel, who calls you by your name." Isaiah 45:2-3*

The book

When the Lord commissioned this book I could not see how it would actually be written or how it would ever come about to be published. You should know that initially, I didn't begin to write a book. I simply started on the adventure of *learning to pray*. Then as the Lord began to teach me and show me the results of deeper prayer, I realized I was a *steward* of these lessons. Have you ever thought about this concept: that some day we will stand before God and give an account of our gifts, our time and even the *truth* that God has placed in our care?

Then came the morning when I heard the instruction from God to focus on this book. He wanted me to turn aside and "work" at this project as if it was my vocation. (It makes me smile that when asked if their mother worked, my kids replied once "Oh no. She doesn't do *anything*.) As the writing came to completion I began to investigate the options for publication. One of the options was to self-publish, which would mean coming up with a sizable about of money. There was also a deadline, if the book was to be prepared in time for the Christian Booksellers Convention. Some significant moments happened as the "flesh" died and the inner man was strengthened that I want to share with you.

On Feb. 1st of 2003 I had a moment of surrender in my quiet time where I told the Lord that I wanted to be *useful* more than I wanted to be *successful*. It may seem like a little thing, but in my heart I was saying "I'd rather be a quiet tool, than a well-known fool."

As the deadline for the manuscript quickly approached my flesh wanted to see the project done in a certain way and on a certain timetable. But in a quiet time on Feb. 7th, I promised the Lord that I would trust HIS way. I wouldn't move ahead without His signals. I would be still and wait for specific marching orders. Like Henry Blackaby's description of Abraham laying Isaac on the altar: "All known possibilities for a future, as far as human reasoning can understand it, were asked to be handed over. If there is to be a future, only God could reveal it."

At our Saturday night prayer time on the 8th of February I was resigned to God's timetable, but felt little *hope*. I quietly called out to the Lord to give me confidence that His way really would be the best way, not just the right way. In other words, the ability to trust His method completely. Unless you have laid your dreams, like a child, on the altar and lifted the knife, you may not understand the intense spiritual victories that were accomplished during this time period in my heart.

On Feb. 10th, I asked the Lord to show me HOW to pray about the details of the book. The answer came the very next day as I was reading about the feeding of the 5,000. This miracle is recorded in each of the four gospels and the Lord gave me insight into my situation through the study of each one. Briefly, I saw how the Lord commanded Philip and the other disciples when He said, "You give them something to eat." We then see the disciples get "off track" in their thinking. They are stumbled by the fact that they don't have food. They don't have enough money. There's even some thought that if they did have enough money... "Would this be something worth spending it on?"

The idea of God requiring the disciples to come up with enough to feed over 5,000 men (plus women and children) is an overwhelming thought. That's when John 6:6 opens up our perspective. We see from this verse that Jesus already knew what He was intending on doing. He already knew HOW it was going to happen. He had the solution before the disciples even faced the problem. But the passage says that he wanted to "test" Philip so he let him squirm around in the inadequacy of his own resources for a little period of time. Then the Holy Spirit opened up one of the most powerful truths I have ever learned from God's Word. When Jesus commanded the disciples with the words, "You give them something to eat," He was authorizing the ability and the resources to get it done. Just the fact that they were commanded to do it was enough to know that it would be done.

Right after this incident occurs, Jesus sends the disciples across the Sea of Galilee to the other side. On the way they are caught in a terrible storm and begin to panic. Gary Smalley opened our insight here (in his video series on marriage), as he relayed that the disciples had no reason to be afraid, because Jesus **had told them to go over to the other side.** Knowing that they had been commanded to cross the lake should have given them peace in the midst of the storm. They were rebuked when panic set in. Jesus said they had not gained any insight from the loaves and fishes. God Almighty stands ready with His ability as we move to complete His will. His commands are His will. Whenever we line ourselves up with His will, we have the benefit of His power behind us.

After this truth was opened up to me in regards to the book I can honestly say that I had a total peace about how, when and in what way the book would finally be published. After all, He told me to write it. He already knows how "it will be done."

On Feb. 17th word came that an anonymous donor had taken care of the expenses of publishing this book. I stood speechless at the thought.

"Such knowledge is too wonderful for me; it is too high, I cannot attain to it." Psalm 139:6

4

Paying Back the Enemy

Look around our world and you'll see plenty that would make God angry. It is not difficult to imagine the pain caused in our Gentle Shepherd's heart when innocent lives are snared, derailed and abused by the evils of pornography, abortion and violence. Can you imagine the disappointment of our detail oriented Creator as he watches His precious creations consumed by drugs, alcohol and suicide? The Source of all wisdom, authority and power stands by as we, with our self will, follow the lies and seduction of His evil arch enemy, the devil. The God of perfect holiness watches as Satan mars the masterpiece of humanity with the graffiti of lust, greed and self-centeredness. His majestic power boils like the internal forces of a volcano at the thought, but His desire for true devotion restrains His omnipotent abilities. *("Who can stand before His indignation? Who can endure the burning of His anger? His wrath is poured out like fire, and the rocks are broken up by Him." Nahum 1:6)*

I love the fact that our Creator feels emotion. His heart aches, like ours does, at pain inflicted on innocence. His anger is stirred, like ours is, at injustice. And His wrath smolders at the one, who attempts to steal, kill and destroy His greatest treasure: His precious children.

Recently, I enjoyed studying Numbers chapter thirty-one during my quiet time. The chapter concerns the children of Israel who have been in the wilderness for forty years and have endured the consequences of their disbelief long enough. It's just about time for God to take Moses home and the Lord gives him one last important task to complete: "Take full vengeance...on the Midianites." This is not just going to be a battle. It's going to be a massacre because God is absolutely fed up. He's seen His people snared by these idol worshippers long enough. He's witnessed enough carnage as a result of His precious peoples "joining themselves" to the world and its destructive ideologies. And at this point in time the Israelites could have gone into battle armed with feathers and still won because God was going to release His wrath on His enemies. (Just a note to you seniors: God used Moses at age 120 to "go to war." In prayer we all have the same potential to "fight" the enemy. Physical strength is no advantage.)

Moses, having seen the promised land from a distance, and realizing that he would never taste the wine made from those beautiful grapes, was a good tool for God to use. He had seen the effects of sin that had robbed his own life of a dream. I believe that with zeal and vengeance aimed in the right direction (at the enemy, not God's people) that Moses carried out God's plans that day.

How does it feel to see a promise, but never taste it? Have you seen the enemy rip off members of your family? Have you witnessed him distracting their attention from God and wasting their giftedness? Have you seen the innocent of this world become prey for Satan's ugly campaigns? Do you wish you could get back at Satan for all the heartache and sorrow he's inflicted? It is my hope that you will discover

HOW to do this through prayer. In the arena of the spiritual, a bedridden grandma can marshal a legion. (All you grandmas out there, get on your combat boots!) You can spend time with God in the quietness of your home and without having to board a plane, learn a second language or get a visa, affect the spread of the gospel on the other side of the globe. (Get the gospel out TODAY by turning aside with Him.) Your entreaties can add sentries to guard and protect God's people. Your cries for God's intervention can stop the internal bleeding in the body of Christ. You don't even have to know where the wounds are to be involved in their healing. (Pick up the scalpel of intercession and remove the tumors of hypocrisy, idolatry and sensuality that drain the life out of God's church.) When you come on your face before the Most High with the same zeal and vengeance of Moses, God, with His sleeves rolled up and His resources readied, will meet you and say: "MAKE MY DAY!"

It's similar in some ways to the story of Samson. Here's a man with great potential for God. A vessel, consecrated and set aside for God's holy use who ends up being the devil's tin can kicked around in the Philistine's back alley for far too long. Looking at Samson chained and blind, treading like an animal, when he had been created to roar like a lion must have broken God's heart. So when Samson prays this prayer: "O Lord God, please remember me and please strengthen me just this time, O God, that I may at once be avenged of the Philistines for my two eyes," (Judges 16:2b), his request coincides with the plans of God and his request is answered by supernatural strength and power.

When Jezebel slays the prophets of the Lord and murders Naboth to get his garden, she probably thought that God didn't even notice. But we see from His Word that not only did He notice, He decided right then and there to make sure the inhabitants of Jezreel knew that He was paying attention to their unjust behavior. He puts in motion this queen's demise and he handpicks Jehu to be the instrument of His revenge. Life goes on for years without any action on God's part. Then Elijah receives instructions to anoint Jehu as king privately. Again, years pass. Then Elisha receives instructions to anoint Jehu as king publicly and within a few days the land of Judah changes drastically. Bam! God puts in motion the removal of Jezebel and her idols. One day the people have nation-wide idol worship, but by nightfall all that are left are true worshippers of the Most High God!

When we get to know God through His Word we see the real God, not just the one we like to imagine. The real God hates evil and gets angry at the waste of human lives. So if we could peer into His mind right now and see His reaction to the condition of our world, I think He'd be seeing RED. Read these verses that describe God's state of mind as He prepares to judge a Christ-rejecting world.

Get to know a new aspect of God's character through His Word: *"**Vengeance is Mine**, and retribution, in due time their foot will slip; for the day of their calamity is near, and the impending things are hastening upon them." Deuteronomy 32:35 "If I sharpen My flashing sword, and My hand takes hold on justice, **I will render vengeance on My adversaries**, and I will repay those who hate Me. Rejoice, O nations, with His people; **for He will avenge the blood of His servants**, and will render vengeance on His adversaries, and will atone for His land and His people." Deuteronomy 32:41, 43 "Say to those with anxious heart, 'Take courage, fear not. Behold, your God will come with vengeance; **the recompense of God will come**, but He will save you." Isaiah 35:4 "And He put on righteousness like a breastplate, and a helmet of salvation on His head; and He put on **garments of vengeance** for clothing, and wrapped Himself with zeal as a mantle." Isaiah 59:17 "**A jealous and avenging God** is the Lord; the Lord is avenging and wrathful. The Lord takes* *vengeance on His adversaries,* **and He reserves wrath for His enemies.**" *Nahum 1:2*

The physical slaughter of the Midianites is just a picture, a symbol, of the spiritual destruction God wants us to inflict on Satan and his demons. I remember preparing to teach a convention seminar on prayer and I had just meditated on Nahum 1:2 (quoted above). As I was praying, out of my mouth popped the words "Lord please let me have revenge on my enemy... for all the lives he's destroyed, for all the lies Satan's told that your people have believed...Please empower me for this moment in time. Let me put the power tools of prayer in the hands of these people so that they will trample him down like the dust." I can assure you that God did just that. I felt His supernatural peace and power flow onto those who listened that day.

Do you know that every day God is looking for people whose greatest desire is to inflict pain on his archenemy? You can just be treading through your day, like Samson, and utter the quietest of prayers, and in response to your heart's cry the fortress of the enemy can be brought down on his head. This cannot be accomplished by your own human abilities. No man could have pulled down the pillars that supported the huge Philistine temple. But God, when steamed up and ready to roar, is looking for a vessel ready to go to war for him. This kind of battle is fought in prayer. It's the kind of battle we fight when we get up in the middle of the night, or pause in the middle of the day and say something like this to the Lord: "I want to wreak havoc on the enemy right now Lord. I don't even know how to word my prayer. But You know where he's working. You know how he's trying to deceive. You know what he's trying to destroy. You know how to aim my prayer, like a bullet, at his plans. Please open up strength, resources and victory for the battle today." God smiles and aims His omnipotent power (like a cannonball) at the enemy's camp.

God used Jehu to destroy the worship of Baal in Israel. What evil would He like to use you to end or destroy? Is it abortion, pornography or child abuse? He's simply looking for one whose heart is full of "zeal for the Lord" and who is willing to trust in His power to accomplish it. How could Jehu have known that morning that idol worship, which had plagued Israel with trouble, would be demolished in a day? He couldn't have, but God knew it. And God knows right now the plans He has to right the wrongs of our world. What will your response be when God taps you on the shoulder and says, "I want you to be my vessel for change?"

"Then I heard the voice of the Lord, saying, 'Whom shall I send, and who will go for Us?' Then I said, 'Here am I. send me!'" Isaiah 6:8

A small group of people from our church goes regularly to pray and counsel at a local abortion clinic. When you're small in numbers, and you are opposing a multi-million dollar industry, it's important to evaluate your resources in advance. It is always encouraging for us to realize that the same God who helped Jehu wipe out Baal-worship in ONE DAY, is also available to support our weak words with His wisdom. On some occasions God uses us to save a baby's life. But I am not satisfied with that. Every day I am asking Him to bring down the entire industry and to do it in a day (if that's what He wants). Jehu reminds me to ask big because God is just as fed up with the loss of innocent life as I am. So pull the pin with your prayer right now. God is standing by with His arsenal of hand grenades. Let your urging press Him for victories already pre-ordained.

In the New Testament when Jesus sends out the disciples by twos, they return full of joy at what has been accomplished. In their zeal to share Christ they have seen God do things THROUGH THEM that have never happened before. *"And the seventy returned with joy, saying, 'Lord, even the demons are subject to us in Your name.'" (Luke 10:17)* Jesus, who can see what is happening in the spirit realm, tells them that He's been watching the effects of their obedience and faith. *"And He said to them, 'I was watching Satan fall from heaven like lightning'" (Luke 10:1)* The opportunity has been opened up to you and me to have the same effect on Satan and his demons today. Will you, by your prayer today, limit Satan's influence, open resources for the spread of the gospel and open the eyes of pre-Christians to the hope of the world?

5

Dealing With Hurt

In order to be an effective prayer warrior, you may first require a deep healing work of the Holy Spirit. Woundedness can be used by God to tenderize you to His Spirit, but it can also be a deadly weapon deployed by the enemy to leave you paralyzed at crucial times in spiritual warfare. We want to allow the Holy Spirit to sweep our lives and point out any spiritual debris or land mines that might be used by the enemy for purposes of evil. We want the Holy Spirit's healing work to break the bonds of bitterness and the entrapment of unforgiveness. We want Him to release the power of love, grace, honesty and truth so that we can become the mighty commanders of prayer He intends for us to be.

Hurt is one of the most effective weapons Satan has ever discovered. It leaves strong Christians powerless and inactive every day. Not too long ago my husband and I were enjoying a quiet lunch in an outdoor eating establishment. We noticed two burly men who planted themselves at the table next to us. I noticed one wore a shirt from my alma mater, Azusa Pacific University, and I asked him about it. As he replied that his wife had attended there the OTHER man stood up and exclaimed "I know you!" After a few seconds I recognized him as one of the many high school students that had been won to the Lord at a church where I had previously served on staff.

Here it was, twenty years later, and I was anxious to find out what the Lord had been doing in his life. He recounted that early on in his spiritual life he had been asked to teach a junior high class. Mike was an on-fire Christian who had made great progress in Jesus. Not too long after he had begun teaching someone's strong criticism of his smoking habit had inflicted tremendous hurt and pain. He had turned and walked away from church from that day on. As we talked that day I made clear to him that the enemy had ripped him off of twenty years of blessing and growth and suggested he join us next week at the church my husband now pastored. Mike is not alone. Millions of Christians have been waylaid by hurt. Some may still be sitting in the pews, but they are not warring at the altar. They are like the walking dead, impotent and ineffective in their lives and service because of land mines of hurt beneath the spiritual surface of their lives.

In my own life, the hurts I had experienced in ministry were minor ones until one day Satan released a nuclear weapon on me. I was serving in a leadership role and was asked by others in authority to resign. The reasons were vague, the preparation for the meeting limited and the relational follow-up afterwards was non-existent. Over a period of months, I was emotionally sideswiped repeatedly and it took many years of recuperation to reach a point of healing and forgiveness. During this time my walk with the Lord deepened and I found Him to be the ultimate counselor. Jesus could put His finger on the place of hurt in a millisecond. His eyes could detect envy and a damaged self-esteem carefully camouflaged under servanthood and good deeds. His mercy could soothe the roughness of injustice and at the same time cleanse the second hand sin, which resulted from the boomerang of hurt.

Do you think there are some areas in your life that the Holy Spirit wants to begin His healing work on so that you can be greatly used by God? Pause here in your reading to ask the Holy Spirit to reveal areas of woundedness in the subterranean parts of your soul. Have there been hurtful words that have marred the truth of who you are in Christ? Have there been situations where the enemy has tried to convince you of your uselessness and valuelessness? If you have pen and paper available write down each scar as they are pointed out by the Lord Jesus Himself. Begin the healing adventure by asking Jesus for a full and complete recovery from these destructive situations. Instantaneous healing is definitely possible, but with emotional hurt, more often than not, the Lord Jesus walks us through a healing *process* so that we can be guides to others on this treacherous path. Once you have discovered and followed the spiritual road markers in His Word you will know the way to the place of healing and be able to point others who are lost or stuck along the way. Jesus is as interested in your life-long usefulness as a tour guide as He is in you taking the journey as a tourist yourself.

> *"Who comforts us in all our affliction so that we may be able to comfort those who are in any affliction with the comfort with which we ourselves are comforted by God." II Corinthians 1:4*

Although everyone deals with hurt during his life, some elements combined with hurt can make it more devastating. It hurts if no one knows exactly what you're going through and you can't explain it. It hurts if you can't talk about it with people you love. And it hurts if you can't escape the place of hurting. Sometimes we see all three of these elements come together in "ministry" situations. This can compound the effect of the hurt, and left untreated, can fester for years.

My own experiences led me to study Biblical examples of those whose lives were marked by scars incurred when dealing with people. I found God's Word to be a textbook on the effects of unresolved relational conflict and its effects on the lives of men and women who love God.

As I studied all the interpersonal conflict David went through I was surprised at the wagon load of anger he dealt with from others...his older brother Eliab, Saul, Michal, his sons, etc. But I am glad God records each difficult entry. It helps me to know that I am not alone in my circumstances. **God wants us to see that even though David was a man after God's own heart that it didn't prevent him from being the target of jealousy from out-of-fellowship believers.** Over the years I'm sure thousands have been helped and encouraged by David's transparency in conflict. We can find every emotion represented in the Psalms. He had a great heart for God, but his life was no picnic. I believe God allowed David's hurt so that his struggle would be chronicled for us. It is easier to view the battle of human emotion and spiritual Lordship played out like a chess game in someone else's life. It's easier to call the plays when you're not on the board yourself. It is interesting to think that the conflicts we deal with are the journals that future generations will read. They will not be inspired Scripture, but they will be living maps that can identify spiritual quick sand for others to avoid and helpful tools for those bent on an upward climb.

Why did Job have to go through all the junk he endured?

So we would know that sometimes God allows horrible stuff "without cause" and so that in "unsparing pain" we would learn not to deny His Lordship. I loved reading about the outcome of Job's suffering. It taught me that trials of hurt could lead to the destination of a triple blessing. It taught me that when others around me are suffering, I can do more good by sitting down with them in silence, than I can by spouting all I know about God. Job showed me that even when I think I haven't done anything wrong, the confidence of my integrity can stink before a Holy God. He encourages me to trust a God wise enough to know all the answers to the quiz He gives Job at the end of the testing.

Why did Joseph have to go through all the stuff he went through?

So we could see that there is a way to get through it all without becoming bitter and resentful. So you and I would see that there is a way to deal with "compounding hurts" over years of time. Joseph didn't just deal with one injustice, he dealt with a series of hurts inflicted by several different people over a period of many years. He was hurt emotionally by the rejection of his brothers. His boss, whom he had worked with for many years, questioned his morality. Then, just when he could believe that he was finally "safe" (for *who* would believe you could be emotionally wounded in a *prison cell*), a fellow sufferer let him down. Remember how the butler made him a sacred promise to "remember him" and then forgot him for two whole years? We see a man who felt deeply the pain of hurt. We discover in Genesis 45:2 that when Joseph finally revealed himself to his brothers, he wept so loudly that all of Pharaoh's household heard it. That's pain! Yet in his cries of woundedness we hear yieldedness. In his wailing we hear waiting. In his pain we hear the unmistakeable sound of forgiveness. Like coins tucked one by one in a piggy bank, those right choices of obedience developed into a treasure all their own, and many years later Joseph would reap the benefits from his submission

Why did Jesus have to go through all He suffered?

So our stuff wouldn't look so hard. Hebrews says that Jesus obeyed "to the point of shedding blood." He sweat drops of blood as He bore our sin. He bore the greatest physical pain and simultaneously, the heaviest relational load, which was separation from His Father. His level of suffering included bearing blasphemous assaults on a perfectly holy character. (He couldn't even rag on the Pharisees after a day of insults, because His own holiness couldn't abide gossip, bitterness or revenge.) When He picked up the bowl and towel to wash each disciple's feet, He found Himself staring rejection and denial in the face. He chose to bend low, and to love them all through service. . Scripture tells us He couldn't do many miracles in His hometown because of unbelief. The small minded stayed the hand of omnipotence and He allowed it because of unconditional love. None of our loads can compare with His.

"For the Lord of Christ <u>overmasters</u> us." II Corinthians 5:14 (Weymouth)

Follow the leader

When I was in Michigan at a family reunion many years ago the young people from our clan decided to hike several miles to some sand dunes for a day of fun. I was younger than my cousin Jean, but much older than the rest of the group. My body was definitely unprepared for the physical journey that lay ahead. The hike was only about 3 miles, but since its path led through sand the trip was much more demanding than a stroll around the block. About halfway there I began to fear that I might not make it. Thank goodness for Jean. She had on a pair of hiking boots and walked ahead of me. I had the advantage of putting my feet in her footprints. This lessened the resistance the sand had on my legs and muscles. I know that without her pre-stamped trail I would not have been able to endure the trip.

So it is with the hurts we bear. We follow our Guide. We place our feet, one by one, in the prints, (the way and manner in which He leads) and we safely pass by the road markers of maturity that lead to our destination. He will not leave us to fend the hurts alone. He has not left us uninformed about the way to get there. His strong example has left a firm mark that we can easily identify and imitate.

Steps to Healing

The first thing we must do is **admit that we have been run over** (by circumstances, or people, or life). If you had been hit by a bus the following would result:

- You would go to the hospital.
- You would receive treatment for your wounds.
- You would have professionals evaluate the damage.
- You would enlist help from others for basic necessities.
- You would allow time for healing.

When my elderly father fell and broke his shoulder, no one expected him to mow his lawn. We didn't even assume he could go to the bathroom alone. We purchased equipment to assist him. We changed our schedules to be with him. All these were helpful in his recuperation. Yet when we deal with emotional hurt many times no one knows it has even happened. No one can see the damage, only its effects. It is so much harder to treat the invisible. That is why we need to seek and depend on the Holy Spirit. God has specifically given Him to be our resident Comforter, our Counselor and the interpreter of our groans before the Father. What a tremendous gift the Father has given us in Him. He can communicate cries and moans to the Father, and line them up with the perfect will OF the Father. He is our personal trainer in spiritual matters and we must learn to tap into the resources He willingly provides.

Intense prayer for healing is the most effective tool I have found in dealing with the damage of hurt. The Lord has allowed me to recognize some earmarks of emotional hurt in others and to intercede for their restoration. He has shown me that corporate prayer by caring Christian brothers and sisters can be helpful in breaking the bonds of dysfunction, resulting from long-term buried hurt. In this process of healing it is encouraging to realize that the Lord Jesus *Himself* has interceded for us. *"Simon, Simon, behold, Satan has demanded permission to sift you like wheat;* **but I have prayed for you**, *that your faith may not fail; and you, when once you have turned again, strengthen your brothers." (Luke 22:31-32)*

Meditate on the following verses and the hope they introduce into our therapy process.

*"I am benumbed and badly crushed; I groan because of the agitation of my heart. Lord, all my desire is before Thee, and **my sighing is not hidden from Thee**." Psalm 38:8*
"Save me, O God, for the waters have threatened my life; I have sunk in deep mire; and there is no foothold; I have come into deep waters; and a flood overflows me. I am weary with my crying, my throat is parched. My eyes fail while I wait for me God. O God, it is Thou who dost know my folly, and my wrongs are not hidden from Thee. May those who wait for Thee not be ashamed through me, O lord God of hosts. May those who seek Thee not be dismayed through me, O God of Israel." Psalm 69:1-3,5-6

Let God's Word be your counselor

In my own struggle for wholeness I felt like a mountain climber. The special verses God gave me were like the cracks in the side of granite, that I could stick my fingers in to pull myself up to the next level. Sometimes I would climb all day and find that I was only back where I started. But even that felt like progress. Getting over this trial of emotional hurt was my goal, but some days I just had to be grateful that I hadn't fallen into the ravine of depression. This season of my life was so out of character to my normally cheery personality that many around me withdrew. They didn't understand the intense struggle that each day required, nor did they want to get mixed up in anything "messy." I try to remember how alone I felt when I see others going through their wilderness experiences. A fresh remembrance of how much it hurt helps me pick up the phone or drop a note to let them know I'm groaning for them before the Father. What a loving Father we have to let us walk through dark valleys to become beacons of light for others on the path!

God is gracious to allow us to experience this kind of loneliness. He knows how powerful the experience will be when we recognize others who are in it. We will see them from the seashore and swim out to them and carry them, by our prayers, to safety. If you are one of God's leaders you will surely face, sometime or another, an experience where you will have to lean your full weight upon the promises of His Word. It is then that you will find that they are able to bear you up.

Tap into the healing power of God's Word:

"Thy servant meditates on Thy statues; Thy testimonies also are my delight; they are my counselors." Psalm 199:23

"Praise the Lord! How blessed is the man who fears the Lord, who greatly delights in His commandments. His descendants will be mighty on earth. **Light arises in the darkness for the upright.***" Psalm 112:1-2,4a "But He knows the way I take; when He has tried me, I shall come forth as gold. My foot has held fast to His path. I have kept His way and not turned aside.* **I have not departed from the command of His lips; I have treasured the words of His mouth more than my necessary food.***" Job 23:10-12*

View yourself as a drink offering

Caution: This instruction should be taken with discernment. It is not meant to be a permission slip for accepting bizarre and destructive behavior from others, but as a sweet smelling method of response to the hurt we do experience from people all around us.

A drink offering was poured out before the Lord. It couldn't be eaten or used like other offerings. It might have been wine, expensive perfume or even water, but it had no other purpose than to be poured out before the Lord. It might have even been viewed as a waste. Judas had this opinion when a woman poured out perfume on Jesus' feet. David offers up a drink offering when his mighty men broke through the enemy lines to get him some well water. The cost of that "bottled water" is too great for David to drink. He pours it out in sacred worship before the Lord. But Paul uses this illustration to view his life in ministry. He is willing to be used up and given away for the sake of those he loves. If Christ can receive more glory through the using up of his life than through the life itself, then Paul is willing to be poured out for others.

A life that loves God more than life is powerful. Think of Joan of Arc. Think of William Tyndale. Think of James

Elliot. We read in Revelation 12:11 *"And they overcame him because of the blood of the Lamb and because of the word of their testimony,* **and they did not love their life even to death.***"* Your days on earth are a commodity that can be used up and given away for others. But God's seed through our lives, when consecrated to Him is guaranteed to bear fruit. We read in John 12:24: *"Truly, truly, I say to you, unless a grain of wheat falls into the earth and dies, it remains by itself alone; but if it dies, it bears much fruit."* Sometimes our death can produce a greater harvest than our life.

"But even if I am being poured out as a drink offering upon the sacrifice and service of your faith, I rejoice and share my joy with you all." Philippians 2:17

"For I am already being poured out as a drink offering, and the time of my departure has come." II Timothy 4:6

Stay clean in the ketchup war and learn to sort your own laundry

In trying to explain to our church staff how difficult it is to get through the spiritual warfare and emotional conflict that hundreds of people can bring to a single service, I explained that it's like wearing white while each person squirts ketchup bottles across the room. Your goal is to cross the room and keep your spiritual garment "white." (This sounds like an actual game some youth pastor might have concocted.) When you are hurting you are not alone. There are lots of other people coming to church who are hurting too. We want to make it to the altar of worship without gossip, without inappropriate expressions of anger, without fear, and without selfish manipulation (to name a few popular ketchup labels). We learn that we are only responsible for our own sin. Nothing that is squirted towards us will stick unless we choose to *participate* in that sin. Even when we fall prey to sin its stains can be removed from our robe during the battle if sin is confessed and forsaken. It is possible to get through the trial with a clean garment, but it will not be easy. It will require moment by moment attention to our own state of cleanliness.

When you feel alone in your circumstance you can't afford to have any distance between you and your Heavenly Father. Make sure that each day you are examining your responses and words for impurities. Acknowledge what is your "sin" and sort what belongs to others into their pile. Like laundry, deal with the stains in your own pile and leave the soils of others for them to deal with.

Meditate on the following verses: *"For our proud confidence is this, the testimony of our conscience, that in holiness and godly sincerity, not in fleshly wisdom, but in the grace of God, we have conducted ourselves in the world, and especially toward you." II Corinthians 1:12 "But as for me, I shall walk in my integrity; redeem me, and be gracious to me." Psalm 26:11 "O Lord my God, if I have done this, if there is injustice in my hands, if I have rewarded evil to my friend, if I have plundered him who without cause was my adversary, let the enemy pursue my soul and overtake it. And let him trample my life down to the ground and lay my glory in the dust." Psalm 7:3-5 "No good thing does He withhold from those who walk uprightly." Psalm 84:11b "All this has come upon us, but we have not forgotten Thee, and we have not dealt falsely with Thy covenant. Our heart has not turned back, and our steps have not deviated from Thy way." Psalm 44:17*

Watch your mouth for bitterness, complaining and gossip

Hurt people hurt other people. Be aware that when you are hurting most you are the least capable of spiritual sight and hearing. Beware lest you think you can be hurt and not fall prey to the enemy's desire to make you sin with your tongue. When you are smarting from emotional pain you need to be careful when talking on the phone or going out to lunch with close friends. Like an alcoholic hanging around a bar you WILL fall. Be smart, run to the Lord. Uncover your "owies" and let Him pour on the oil and re-bandage your wounds for you. *(Note: Isolation can also be a tool of the enemy when we are hurting.)*

Plant these truths in your heart to protect you from sins of the mouth: *"Do not let any unwholesome talk come out of your mouths, but only what is helpful for building others up according to their needs, that it may benefit those who listen." Ephesians 4:29 NIV "Keep your tongue from evil, and your lips from speaking deceit. Depart from evil and do good. Seek peace and pursue it." Psalm 34:13-14 "I said, 'I will guard my ways that I may not sin with my tongue. I will guard my mouth as with a muzzle.'" Psalm 39:1a*

Weed your heart often to keep out roots of bitterness and anger

At one point I was dealing with hurt and at the same time studying two verses in I Peter that seemed to contradict each other. One verse said I was to love others from the heart and the other said I was to be without hypocrisy. I wondered how the truths of both verses could be evident in my life. If I was to really show love to those who had hurt me, there might have to be a shell of hypocrisy. If I was to love from the heart no hypocrisy could be allowed. I cried out to the Lord to show me how to live both verses at the same time. The Lord gave me the picture of a garden. He pointed out that you can only pull up one-day's worth of weeds. You can't make sure another weed will never grow, and you can't weed ahead of time. But when you see a weed, you are to pull it up immediately. In the same way Jesus encouraged me to be on the look out for the weeds of bitterness and hypocrisy. Both destroy the beauty of His gardening in my life.

"Cease from anger, and forsake wrath; Do not fret, it leads only to evildoing." Psalm 37:8 "My little children, let us not love in word or in tongue, but in deed and in truth. And by this we know that we are of the truth and shall assure our hearts before Him." I John 3:18-19

Remind yourself that God loves you and hears your prayers

When we pray for something over a long period of time it's hard to stay encouraged, especially if we don't see any progress on the answer. I was thirty-four and still single, yet I had prayed for years for the Lord to bring me my prince. One morning in my quiet time I was whining to the Lord about His lack of effort on this particular request when all of a sudden the Holy Spirit conveyed a mental picture that silenced my pity.

The idea was that every time I had prayed and asked the Lord to work on this particular need, that He had responded with little bits of action and love (like someone putting together a big surprise party for a friend). And here I was a few weeks before *the party* whining that no one cared about me. All the time the Lord had been making out invitations, ordering the cake, etc. Every time I had asked the Lord to prepare a prince for me He had heard my prayer, and had put into motion the steps that would eventually lead to my meeting the wonderful man who is now my husband. Every cry from my heart had sent angelic couriers into motion with details to attend to... but it wasn't quite time for the big party. And here I was whining that no one ever did anything for ME.

When I began to act on that knowledge, that God had responded to every one of these requests, my whining turned to praise. "I know you've been working God," I would say with a smile. "You've been listening and orchestrating." "Thank you Lord." It was about six weeks later that my husband and I met. (What a celebration our wedding was!)

Dealing with hurt and healing takes a lot of time. But I hope that as you pray for a complete restoration of heart and soul that you will keep the picture of God's surprise party in mind. Every time you ask for healing of your damaged emotions He pulls out the party streamers and begins to hang them up. Every time you struggle with revengeful thoughts and plead for more mercy to forgive, He blows up the balloons. And some day it will be time for the celebration of complete healing in your life. Know that it's already in the works.

Focus on truth as you experience the pain: *"But know that the Lord has set apart the godly man for Himself; the Lord hears when I call to Him. Tremble and do not sin, meditate in your heart upon your bed and be still. Offer the sacrifices of righteousness and trust in the Lord." Psalm 4:3-5 "Many are saying of my soul, 'There is no deliverance for him in God.' But Thou, O Lord, art a shield about me. My glory, and the One who lifts my head. I was crying to the Lord with my voice, and He answered me from His holy mountain. I lay down and slept; I awoke, for the Lord sustains me. I will not be afraid of ten thousands of people who have set themselves against me round about." Psalm 3:2-6 "I will cry to God most High, to God who accomplishes all things for me. He will send from heaven and save me."*

Psalm 57:2 "Behold, the eye of the Lord is on those who fear Him, on those who hope for lovingkindness, to deliver their soul from death, and to keep them alive in famine. Our soul waits for the Lord; He is our help and our shield. For our heart rejoices in Him because we trust in His holy name, let Thy lovingkindness, O Lord, be upon us, according as we have hoped in Thee." Psalm 33:18-22 "Thou hast seen it, O Lord, do not keep silent; O Lord, do not be far from me. Stir up Thyself and awake to my right and to my cause, my God and my Lord." Psalm 35:22-23 "For the Lord has heard the voice of my weeping. The Lord has heard my supplication. The Lord receives my prayer. All my enemies shall be ashamed and greatly dismayed; they shall turn back, they shall suddenly be ashamed." Psalm 6:8b-10

Keep focusing on God's goodness and work backwards what you don't understand

Do you remember learning about the unknown factor in math? You had to find out what number went in that empty box. "Something plus this number equals the other number," you were told. Sometimes when we get handed a lot of hurt, it's hard to think that a pile of manure could ever become something good in our lives. It's then that we have to do what we learned to do in math. We have to work backwards. Something plus God's goodness equals good for me. We don't understand what goes in the box, but we work backwards from what we know. Start with what you are sure of: God is good and God works all things for my good. Then no matter what the enemy sticks in the box, you can arrive at a correct conclusion: This will work out for my good.

I learned this concept in the school of hard knocks. One morning I got a call from another Christian school in town. They had collected books to raise money for one of their students who needed heart surgery. Because they had more books than they needed, they were willing to give them to OUR school. I drove over, filled my car and headed over to our library, where our smiling librarian met me. She sorted through the volumes and took out all we could use. There were still lots of books left. We were surprised by the content of some of these books. Many were dime store novels that seemed inappropriate for Christians to have, let alone donate to a Christian school. It was suggested that we take them to a used bookstore for credit on GOOD books. It made sense at the time, but later my husband said I should have just put them in the dumpster. How I wish I had done that very thing!

I had never been to this bookstore before. I was straining to find the location when all of a sudden I saw it out of the corner of my eye. The street seemed deserted so I made an extra wide left turn that sort of turned into a U-turn. In doing so I caused my first and only accident. But it was a doo-sy. I hit, if you can believe this, a POLICE OFFICER on a MOTORCYCLE. If you are going to have an accident there are lots of better ways to do it than to BE AT FAULT, TO HIT A PERSON, TO HIT A COP, TO HIT HIM ON A MOTORCYCLE, and TO DO IT ON THE MAIN STREET IN YOUR TOWN. What's worse is having your husband be the police chaplain and to have to tell him from a squad car that the back of your car and the trunk are full of "smutty books." After the officer was taken to the hospital (where he was later released with only a few minor injuries) and I was questioned (the officer said it was refreshing to have someone admit they were totally at fault), I went home. It was a dark day emotionally. I didn't want to see anyone. I was devastated. As I sat in my living room talking to the Lord about this horrible, no good, very bad day He took the time to remind me about Romans 8:28.

After the Holy Spirit had reminded me of its promise and assured my heart that SOMEHOW even this event qualified to be used for good, I felt a little better. There were consequences to my poor driving choice. I had to pay higher insurance, go without a car for about six weeks, take cookies to the injured officer and face a lot of good-natured ribbing about my car's picture on the front page of the paper. But in the end God had the last laugh. When my mother saw me getting up at five in the morning to take my husband to the church for prayer so I could have a car to drive, she generously gave our family the nicest car we have ever owned. My father had passed away. My mother no longer needed a car. So now as I sat on beautiful leather seats and pushed buttons to do almost everything but give myself a manicure I realized that God HAD used this, a horrible accident, to bless me and my family.

A policeman, who attended our church, had been witnessing to the officer I had hit. When I delivered his cookies I added a note with a little humor. I wrote, "I hope you have been thinking about what T____ has been trying to tell you. You need to be prepared for eternity. And with drivers like me out there you might just meet your Maker a little sooner than you think." (Smile.)

"Thank you for this horrible day where I was totally humiliated, because if it wasn't for you... I wouldn't have had <u>a day at all</u>!" Monica (an angel) on the TV show: <u>Touched by an Angel</u>

People can hurt others in such horrible and violent ways. But just about the time we think something like "How could God ever use something this bad?" He pulls up His sleeves and gets to work on it. Weeks, months or years later we have to admit He was right. He has used it to bring about ultimate good in our lives.

This book is the result of the blessing that accompanies hurt and healing. Its truths were birthed in pain, but as a result of yielding within that pain, I am trusting God to use it to bring comfort and help to others.

"The Lord is for me; I will not fear; what can man do to me? You pushed me violently so that I was falling, but the Lord helped me. I shall not die, but live and tell of the works of the Lord. The Lord has disciplined me severely, but He has not given me over to death." Psalm 118:6, 13, 17-18

Prayer journal entry:

9/12/02 I counsel a young woman whose husband has just made a decision to enter the service. This means she and her two children will be away from him for months. She does not have a peace about it. She will be living with her parents during his boot camp. She is not happy. She does not see God's hand in the circumstances.

12/02 I get an email from this same woman. The separation has been very difficult, but after spending Christmas together she sees a tremendous growth that has taken place in her husband. She is thanking the Lord for His help.

Focus on God's good purposes for you: *"Because they did not believe in God, and did not trust in His salvation. But He led forth His own people like sheep and guided them in the wilderness like a flock." Psalm 78:22,52 "Why are you in despair, O my soul? And why have you become disturbed within me? Hope in God, for I shall again praise Him for the help of His presence." Psalm 42:5 "'For my thoughts are not your thoughts, neither are your ways my ways,' declares the Lord. 'For as the heavens are higher than the earth, so are my ways higher than your ways and my thoughts than your thoughts.'" Isaiah 55:8-9*

Keep an eye on the rearview mirror of life

It is always easier to trust the Lord when you can look backwards through time. If we can keep an eye on the rearview mirror of life, we can see that those things, which are hard to understand, become clearer with time. There are hundreds of stories I could use to illustrate this point. I am going to use an incident that occurred in the final days of my father's life.

In December of 2000, he was diagnosed with pancreatic cancer. This did not come as a shock to our family. Dad had been rapidly losing weight and his doctor at that time was too busy to give his case the attention it deserved. When dad changed insurance carriers a new doctor quickly assessed the problem, but the cancer was too far-gone for treatment. It was just a matter of time before my dad would pass away. Knowing this, we treasured the times we shared. My father had always been a great influence on my life. We shared common passions and personalities. So each hour we could sit and talk was a gift from the Lord. The Lord also blessed Dad with another gift. He never experienced pain. Up to the day he died, his pain medication (left by the hospice doctor) remained unopened. (This cancer can be the most painful. He felt that God gave him this miracle because he was such a baby about pain.)

As the end drew near and Daddy got weaker and weaker, he began choking whenever he took a sip of water. This was so difficult to watch. He needed to moisten his dry mouth, but the water would cause so much discomfort it was hard to even give it to him. The last weekend of his life (he died two days after his seventy-eighth birthday) was the hardest. His tenderhearted family longed to have the Lord take him home and yet the Lord did not. We watched him suffer through the choking and wondered "Why?" There are so many times in our lives and in our praying that we come to this question.

So many times things happen in an unexpected way. But remember we evaluate each situation in light of the character of God. God loves. He cares. Even this pain could be used for His good.

The following Monday Mom and I were near his bed. He was resting, but still conscious. In came his hospice nurse, Tammy. She was surprised to see that her patient had survived the weekend. We were still wondering why the Lord had allowed this suffering to continue. But we soon knew the answer. Tammy came over to his bed and began to pour out her heart. "Thank you Pastor Herb. Thank you so much for what you told me to do about my marriage." (Dad was a pastor until the day he died. Here Tammy thought she was caring for a patient, but Dad was doing marriage counseling from his deathbed.) She went on, "We got away this weekend and just had a lot of time to talk and be together. And Pastor Herb, it worked. Thank you so much. I was just hoping the Lord would let me tell you thank you." Dad smiled a peaceful smile and we all knew why God had allowed his coughing and suffering for one more weekend. Dad had been assigned one more chance to serve and make a difference in a life forever. Dad peacefully passed away two days later.

It was nice to have the comfort of knowing "WHY" so quickly, but the answers don't always come like that. There are sometimes years and decades (even longer) where we are stuck in the waiting and the "why." It is at these times that we need to remember most to trust the Lord. He is a God who cannot lie. His love for us is so very great. His compassion for us is so deep. His eye is on the eternal. His power is great enough to get us through anything.

Bandage your wounds with some of God's *love* **thoughts:** *"But as for me, I would seek God and I would place my cause before God; who does great and unsearchable* *things, wonders without number." Job 4:8-9 "We do not lose heart. Even though our outward man is perishing, yet the inward man is being renewed day by day. For our light affliction, which is but for a moment, is working for us a far more exceeding and eternal weight of glory, while we do not look at the things which are seen, but at the things which are not seen. For the things which are seen are temporary, but the things which are not seen are eternal." II Corinthians 4:16-18 NIV "Blessed be the Lord, who daily loads us with benefits, the God of our salvation!" Psalm 6:19 NKJV "I know that Thou canst do all things, and that no purpose of Thine can be thwarted." Job. 42:2*

Offer the gift of praise and humility as sacrifices

Praising is the hardest thing to do when we are hurting. That's why it's so precious to God. It's like expensive perfume. The reason we feel good wearing it is that it costs so much. When we praise God through our hurt He recognizes the price paid for the gift we give Him and He delights in the aroma.

Let your cries of pain become cries of praise with the help of these verses: *"And He put a new song in my mouth, a song of praise to our God. Many will see and fear, and trust in the Lord." Psalm 40:3 "But as for me, I shall sing of Thy strength; yes, I shall joyfully sing of Thy lovingkindness in the morning, for Thou hast been my stronghold, and a refuge in the day of my distress. O my strength, I will sing praises to Thee; for God is my stronghold, the God who shows me lovingkindness." Psalm 59:16-17 "Deliver me from the mire, and do not let me sink; may I be delivered from my foes, and from the deep waters. May the flood of water not overflow me, and may the deep not swallow me up, and may the pit not shut its mouth on me. Answer me, O*

Lord, for Thy lovingkindness is good; according to the greatness of Thy compassion, turn to me, and do not hide Thy face from Thy servant, for I am in distress; answer me quickly. I will praise the name of God with song, and shall magnify Him with thanksgiving. And it will please the Lord better than an ox or a young bull with horns and hoofs. The humble have seen it and are glad; you who seek God, let your heart revive. For the Lord hears the needy, and does not despise His who are prisoners." Psalm 69:14-17, 30-33

Don't be afraid of being "needy"

It's hard for us to admit our neediness. We are more comfortable behind the façade of competence. But when we are willing to acknowledge our neediness, (like an alcoholic at an AA meeting) we find that we are one step closer to healing than when we denied our helpless condition. After studying so many verses that teach God's closeness to the needy, I realized that what I tended to avoid was actually the treatment I desperately needed. God presence is closest to the broken and the helpless. As long as we tell Him we don't need any help He refrains from giving it to us.

Read about the gifts God gives to all who identify with neediness: *"He raises the poor from the dust and lifts* **the needy** *from the ash heap to make them sit with princes, with the princes of His people." Psalm 113:7-8 "But He sets* **the needy** *securely on high away from affliction and makes his families like a flock. The upright see it and are glad, but all unrighteousness shuts its mouth." Psalm 107:41-42 "But Thou, O God, the Lord, deal kindly with me for Thy name's sake; because Thy loving kindness is good, deliver me; for I am afflicted and* **needy***, and my heart is wounded within me. For He stands at the right hand of* **the needy***, to save him from those who judge his soul." Psalm 109:21-22,31 "***The***

afflicted and needy *are seeking water, but there is none. And their tongue is parched with thirst. I, the Lord, will answer them Myself." Isaiah 41:17 "As the God of Israel, I will not forsake them for thus says the high and exalted One who lives forever, whose name is Holy, 'I dwell on a high and holy place, and* ***also with the contrite and lowly of spirit*** *in order to revive* ***the spirit of the lowly and to revive the heart of the contrite.'** " Isaiah 57:15 NIV*

Identify the real enemy

People may have been involved in the circumstances of your hurt but they are never the real masterminds of the operation. The REAL enemy is no one wearing skin. It's not the person who called to unload on you, your husband, or even your children. Unfortunately though, when you are dealing with emotions or depression, they just happen to be around and we deem them guilty by association. Emotions are messy and spill over like hot gravy onto whoever might be standing by the stove. We have to learn to say, "sorry," when our hurt spills over and wounds others. We have to take responsibility for the results of OUR own words and actions. Mostly, we have to learn where to aim our arrows.

Here are some truths that can focus our attention on our true adversary: *"Consider and answer me, O Lord, my God; enlighten my eyes, lest I sleep the sleep of death, lest my enemy say, 'I have overcome him,' lest my adversaries rejoice when I am shaken." Psalm 13:3-4 "O give us help against the adversary, for deliverance by man is in vain. Through God we shall do valiantly; and it is He who will tread down our adversaries." Psalm 60:11-12 "I will rejoice and be glad in Thy lovingkindness, because; Thou hast seen my affliction. Thou hast known the troubles of my soul, and Thou hast not given me over into the hand of the enemy. Thou hast set my* *feet in a large place." Psalm 31:7-8 "When he aims his arrows, let them be as headless shafts." Psalm 58:7b*

Hide out, as often as necessary, with God

God's office is always open and whenever you are discouraged, overwhelmed or depressed you can walk right in anytime. There are no appointments necessary for YOU. You can put your feet up on His couch, unload and ask Him for some life-changing advice. You will never walk out feeling like you weren't heard and you will never wonder if He understands the *whole* situation. Take advantage of this wonderful relationship you have with the Almighty God of the Universe.

Enjoy a session with the Almighty Counselor: *"For God is with the righteous generation. You would put to shame the counsel of the afflicted; but the Lord is his refuge." Psalm 14:5b-6 "Wondrously show Thy loving kindness. O Savior of those who take refuge at Thy right hand. From those who rise up against them; keep me as the apple of the eye. Hide me in the shadow of Thy wings." Psalm 17:7-8 "Be Thou to me a rock of habitation, to which I may continually come." Psalm 71:3a. "In my distress I called upon the Lord and cried to my God for help. He heard my voice out of His temple and my cry for help before Him came into His ears. For Thou dost light my lamp. The Lord my God illumines my darkness. For by Thee I can run upon a troop and by my God I can leap over a wall." Psalm 18:6, 28-29 "For in the day of trouble He will conceal me in His tabernacle; in the secret place of His tent He will hide me." Psalm 27:5 "Thou art my hiding place, Thou dost preserve me from trouble; Thou dost surround me with songs of deliverance." Psalm 32:7*

Use the time to refocus on your calling, your purpose and your priorities

"What have you called me to do, Lord? What gifts have you given me? What am I doing that I shouldn't be doing, and what must I continue to do no matter what?" These are questions we can ask during a spiritual recuperation period that we don't have time for when we are running around active and well. When hurt makes us stop, we might as well take advantage of the hospital stay and do some long-term evaluation.

"O God, Thou hast taught me from my youth; and I still declare Thy wondrous deeds. And even when I am old and gray, O God, do not forsake me, until I declare Thy strength to this generation." Psalm 71:17-18

"We will not conceal them from their children, but tell to the generation to come the praises of the Lord and His strength and His wondrous works that He has done. That the generation to come might know, even the children yet to be born, that they may arise and tell them to their children. That they should put their confidence in God, and not forget the works of God, but keep His commandments." Psalm 7:4, 6-7

6

Praying Prayers That Get Answered

Sin causes our prayers to have no effect

When we have unconfessed sin in our lives God does not hear our prayers, except for confession. When our lives are clean before Him, by the blood of His Son, we have access to His presence and power. Therefore, careful attention must be given to the state of our souls at all times. Why pray and have our prayers be impotent?

Sin causes us to run away from His presence

The enemy delights in unconfessed sin. It causes us to recognize our shame and hide behind excuses. The devil knows that there is no fellowship found without entering the sin-free presence of God. So as soon as you are aware of your sin, get it taken care of right away. "Search me O

Waiting at the Window

God"... is a good way to begin your time with God.

There are many times I have come into the presence of God and begun my prayer time with the verse, "Search me O God and know my heart." Many times I did it with the subconscious thought that "I think I'm OK today," only to be met immediately by the prompting of the Holy Spirit that I was far from "OK." One Sunday morning I remember glibly spouting those words "Search me O God..." There was little hesitation from the Spirit of God. He immediately put His finger on three incidents that had taken place over twenty years previously. I had never seen the reality of these three situations for what they were, blatant sin. Now I saw how horrid they were and how they had grieved my loving, Holy Father. There was nothing that I could do but sit down and write letters asking for forgiveness. God could never bless my service in worship that day without a response to His revelation.

This was especially difficult since two of the incidents required me to write the leaders of two churches I had served at, and to do so with humiliating honesty. God was not satisfied with just repentance. In two of the three situations, He wanted me to make restitution for the damage my sin might have caused. However, as always happens when we are obedient to the Spirit of God, there was great spiritual power released that day. Also, some baseball bats of guilt that the enemy might have held over my head were taken out of his hands and put in the dumpster.

Here is one of the three things God brought to my attention that morning. At one church where I had served on staff, I had placed a set of flutophone hymn arrangements among MY things and had never returned them to the school when I left. I had to admit the totality of my sin. I had committed thievery and needed to make restitution. (I hope I am never known as the Flutophone Music Bandit.) The person I confessed to allowed me to speak at a school chapel service to "make up the loss" to the organization. The materials were returned and the joy of the Lord became mine once more. If you ever ask the Lord to search your heart for unknown sin you just might be surprised at what He remembers.

"Not only does sin hinder prayer; prayer hinders sin. The two are always opposed. The more careless we are about sin, the less we will pray. The more we pray, the less careless we will be about sin. Both sin and prayer are powerful forces. Which one is moving you?" Dr. Alvin Vander Griend - National Facilitator of Lighthouse Ministries for the Mission America Coalition

"Have one fear, fear to leave Him. Be always with Him. Let us live in His presence. Let us die in His presence." Brother Lawrence

"And they heard the sound of the Lord God walking in the garden in the cool of the day, and the man and his wife hid themselves from the presence of the Lord God among the trees of the garden." Genesis 3:8 "But Jonah rose up to flee to Tarshish from the presence of the Lord. So he went down to Joppa, found a ship which was going to Tarshish, paid the fare, and went down into it to go with them to Tarshish from the presence of the Lord." Jonah 1:3 "Repent therefore and return, that your sins may be wiped away, in order that times of refreshing may come from the presence of the Lord." Acts 3:19

"When I go aside in order to pray, I find my heart unwilling to approach God; and when I tarry in prayer my heart is unwilling to abide in Him. Therefore I am compelled first to pray to God to move my heart into Him, and when I am in Him, I pray that my heart remain in Him." John Bunyan

A different morning, I again asked the Spirit of God to search my heart. I had been praying for the salvation of a family friend and had been reminded in a book by R.A. Torrey that sometimes our prayers are hindered by unconfessed sin. The Lord revealed to me that I had spent twenty-seven dollars on clip art the month before and had never told my husband about it. Now twenty-seven dollars is not that big of a deal, and I had not planned to keep it a secret, but at this very moment it was a secret. It was, as the Holy Spirit pointed out, a wall to the transparency He wanted between my husband and me and it had to be confessed. Quickly I went in and woke my husband and asked for forgiveness. I said, "God can't hear my prayer for _____'s salvation until I tell you that I spent twenty-seven dollars on clip art without telling you." A groggy, but loving husband forgave me, turned over and went back to sleep. I however, went back to the same prayer request with GREAT POWER.

The components to prayer are twofold: the part that only God Almighty controls and the parts I can control. God controls His own perfect will and its timing. I can come to know God's will just as I have come to know my own father's heart. After spending over forty-six years in fellowship with my earthly father, I could tell you after watching a movie if my father would like it or not. (If it was funny and clean he would like it.) I learned this by watching his reactions to many a movie. I learned to read body language, facial expression and comments he made during and after the movie. This education took much time, but because I cared to please my father I was always interested in learning more that would guarantee my choice of movies to be a HIT. It is similar with my Heavenly Father. He has given me many clues of what He likes and dislikes right in His Word. Sometimes He just comes right out and says, "I hate that!" or, "I love that!" Then it's easy. It gets more difficult when the lines are not as distinct, but I can still tell many times by the general principles of His Word. If nothing else, I can ask in my prayer time and get more information through the spiritual response of God's "body language." The Holy Spirit is always quick to show me when God is grieved and I can personally feel His pleasure through His part of the conversation (and an openness from Him to ask for more).

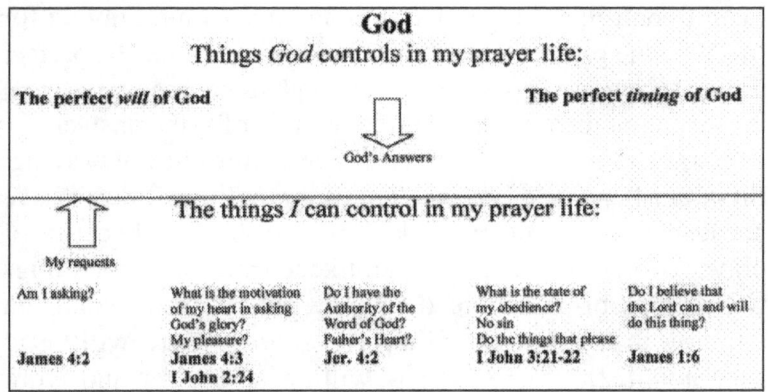

If the request I have isn't the perfect will of God then I really wouldn't want it anyway. One year prior to buying our current home, we were in escrow on what we thought would be our first home. I had just given birth to our first child and we were living out of boxes waiting for the deal to close. Day after day our agent gave excuses for the delay and we were growing impatient living with 90% of the baby equipment packed. As we prayed, my husband said out loud, "Honey, if this isn't God's best then maybe that's why it's not going through." It was hard to let go of our expectations to be in our own home, but we put our trust in a loving Heavenly Father who knew more than we did about it all. We chose to rent a home for one year. At the end of that year we found a house with twice as much square footage for less money. During that twelve months the Lord had lowered the interest rate, just for us we imagined, and got us in for no money down. We came to learn later that this house had sat uninhabited for exactly one year. During that year the representing agent did some things to fix it up to get rid of it. Our home came painted and newly carpeted just because they wanted to MOVE it at just the time we were ready to buy. Isn't God good?

This also illustrates the next part of the prayer process that I can't control: God's perfect timing. What I am praying for MAY be the perfect will of God, but it may not be His perfect timing. God only gives good gifts and sometimes time is an important element to prepare the recipient for the answer.

Now, let's look at the areas I can control in my praying. First, am I asking? James 4:2 says many times I don't have because I simply do not ask. This can happen because of prayer overload. We simply can't keep track of all the things we need to bring before the Lord. This is what makes an ongoing prayer list essential. The more we are willing to pray about, the more God is willing to answer and work through on our behalf. So ask!

When Sennacherib's army surrounds Hezekiah and the land of Judah, Hezekiah heads to the place of answers, the house of God. He lays out Sennacherib's blaspheming words before the Lord. *"Has any one of the gods of the nations delivered his land from the hand of the king of Assyria? Where are the gods of Hamath and Arpad? Where are the gods of Sepharvaim, Hena and Ivvah? Have they delivered Samaria from my hand? Who among all the gods of the lands have delivered their land from my hand, that the Lord should deliver Jerusalem from my hand?" (II Kings 1:33-35)* "Did you hear what he said about You?" is how Hezekiah's prayer began. It turns out that God was listening and decided to bring victory to an impossible situation. He tells Hezekiah WHY He is going to turn the tide: ***"Because you have prayed to Me about Sennacherib*** *king of Assyria, I have heard you." (II Kings 19:20)* Because you brought me this problem I will save you. Doesn't that make you want to ASK God to help in more situations?

Sometimes we view God as a spiritual genie that allocates only three wishes per year. We may be fearful of "using up our quota" thoughtlessly. The more we get to know the expansive wisdom and power of God, the more we realize that the only limitations on HIS abilities are in OUR MIND. Because He can touch and move any circumstance that we are willing to bring to Him, and because His power is not limited or rationed in any way, we can ask freely, without reserve.

Next, I must be willing to have the behind the scenes "motivation" for my request examined. God tells us in James 4:3 that asking for a good thing for a bad reason will not receive an answer. If I want revival so I will have a bigger church, my prayer goes unanswered. If I want my husband saved so that I can have an easier life, I may not see any answer to my prayer. The glory of God is the correct motivation for any prayer I could pray. I want revival because right now my city and nation are not giving the glory due their Creator. "I want my husband to receive Christ," someone might pray, "because he is thumbing his nose at the Almighty God who made Heaven and Earth." These are prayers that will be heard and if they are the will of God (understood by Scripture to be exactly that) and it is the perfect timing for them, they will be answered. As I read R.A. Torrey's thoughts on this subject the Lord gave the chart shown on p. 109. It helped me to see that I am only responsible for MY PART. He is responsible for HIS PART.

Thirdly, I must know if there is any promise or bank note in God's Word that holds Him to granting my request. If I am struggling financially I can remind Him that the children of the righteous are never found begging for bread. If I am praying for someone's salvation I can remind God that He wants none to perish.

Fourthly, I must ask the Holy Spirit to check the state of my heart. Is there any sin that must be confessed to clear up the channel of communication to my Father? If I regard sin in my heart, the Lord will not hear my prayer. But we must go further in this area. R.A. Torrey points out that it is not just avoiding sin that brings answered prayer, but also doing the things that please the Lord (James 2:23) that bring His response. When I do the things I know I should do, this pleases the heart of God and He promises to HEAR MY PRAYER.

"Beloved, if our heart does not condemn us, we have confidence before God; and whatever we ask we receive from Him, because we keep His commandments and do the things that are pleasing in His sight." I John 3:2-22

The final element that can affect my prayer request is simply my belief that God can and will do it. Sometimes the problem is believing that God CAN do something about this situation. It may seem so big and out of reach that I cannot even fathom that God could do anything about it. Or in my mind I may be able to fathom that he CAN do it, but I still may struggle with my belief that He WILL do it. James tells us that we must believe that He is and that He rewards those who seek Him. The second phrase of this verse is the harder part for me to internalize. There really is a connection between loving and serving my Heavenly Father and His blessings in my life. I may need a brain transfusion from His Word to remind me that what I get is different than what I think I deserve. God's blessings for me have more to do with who's picking them out than whom they are for.

*"Then he turned his face to the wall, and prayed to the Lord, saying, '**Remember now, O Lord**, I beseech Thee, **how I have walked before Thee in truth and with a whole heart,***

and have done what is good in Thy sight.' And Hezekiah wept bitterly. And it came about before Isaiah had gone out of the middle court, that the word of the Lord came to him, saying, 'Return and say to Hezekiah the leader of My people, "Thus says the Lord, the God of your father David, **I have heard your prayer, I have seen your tears; behold, I will heal you.** *On the third day you shall go up to the house of the Lord."' " II Kings 20:2-5*

"And Elijah answered and said to the captain of fifty, **'If I am a man of God, let fire come down from heaven and consume you and your fifty.'** *Then fire came down from heaven and consumed him and his fifty." II Kings 1:10, 12*

Corporate Cleanness

Sometimes my heart is clean, but I am in a corporate setting where there is unconfessed sin. It may be my child, my friend or my neighbor who has disobeyed God, but it can still guarantee defeat in battle. He sniffs out the Achans among us in an instant. (See Joshua 7 for how God searches out secret sin.) If we want corporate prayer power, then we must learn to seek corporate cleanness of heart. This can be done by a get down to business time at the altar before communion where the people are instructed that we are going "no farther" until all hearts are at rest before the Lord. The Corinthian church experienced this problem. They were choosing to ignore blatant sin in their midst and God held them accountable for it.

Remind yourself of how God feels about ignoring sin: *"It is actually reported that there is immorality among you, and immorality of such a kind as does not exist even among the Gentiles, that someone has his father's wife. And you have become arrogant, and have not mourned instead, in* *order that the one who had done this deed might be removed from your midst." I Corinthians 5:1-2 "Or do you not know that the unrighteous shall not inherit the kingdom of God? Do not be deceived; neither fornicators, nor idolaters, nor adulterers, nor effeminate, nor homosexuals, nor thieves, nor the covetous, nor drunkards, nor revilers, nor swindlers, shall inherit the kingdom of God." I Corinthians 6:9-10 "But because of your stubbornness and unrepentant heart you are storing up wrath for yourself in the day of wrath and revelation of the righteous judgment of God." Romans 2:5*

National Cleanness

There is another aspect of God's character that must be considered here: His justice. How could he destroy Sodom and Gomorrah and yet overlook the homosexuality in America? How could he be upset with the Midianites because of their idol worship and overlook the god of money that is worshipped every day in our country? How can we think that He could hold the elders responsible for the death on an innocent person found **near** their city and let us off the hook for the millions of babies slaughtered every year by abortion? (Read about this in Deuteronomy 21.) There is much to get on our knees and say "sorry" for.

"So you shall remove the guilt of innocent blood from your midst, when you do what is right in the eyes of the Lord." Deuteronomy 21:9

The importance of a clean heart in battle

*"When you go out as an army against your enemies, then you **shall keep yourself from every evil thing**." Deuteronomy 23:9*

We live near a city where many people keep horses. A good friend from our church has several, as well as dogs, cats, chickens, etc. One day when we were walking on his property he casually told me to "watch my step." It was good advice. There were many piles lying around of the kind of stuff you don't want on your clean shoes. When I read the following verse I realized that sometimes people tell God to "watch His step." A holy God might just wander into some dung laying around in our lives. But God tells His people that they had better use His "pooper scooper" because if He finds uncleanness, He leaves camp (taking His victory power with Him.)

*"Since the Lord your God walks in the midst of your camp to deliver you **and to defeat your enemies before you**, therefore your camp must be holy; and **He must not see anything indecent among you lest He turn away from you**." Deuteronomy 23:14*

Clean Conversation

"Let no unwholesome word proceed from your mouth, but only such a word as is good for edification according to the need of the moment, that it may give grace to those who hear." Ephesians 4:29

Clean Conscience

"I thank God, whom I serve with a clear conscience the way my forefathers did, as I constantly remember you in my prayers night and day." II Timothy 1:3 "And keep a good conscience so that in the thing in which you are slandered, those who revile your good behavior in Christ may be put to shame." I Peter 3:16

Clear of Relational Discord

Sometimes it is not even sin that keeps our prayers unheeded. It is simply relational disharmony that clouds the reception with static. It was a Sunday morning and there was a hurricane of emotion going on in our car on the way to church. My daughter had pushed the buttons of disobedience and I had just informed her that she would not be going to the beach later that day. Our church always had beach baptisms at least one time each summer. She was angry. I was frustrated. We both walked into church. She headed towards her Sunday school class and I into the worship service. Wouldn't you know it? That Sunday was to be a time of communion. As the elements were passed out I knew that I was not in any way able to partake without patching up our earlier argument. Although I didn't believe my actions had crossed the line into sin's territory, there was disharmony between us and I knew God couldn't bless us in that condition. So while they were praying I slipped out and got my daughter out of class. We had a tender time of restoration in the hallway. I walked back into the service and took communion with a full and clean heart. The rest of the day was packed with spiritual power.

You see, if the enemy can get you to try to serve the Lord with unclean hands, he has won the battle on many different levels. The enemy always tries to cause conflict just before a church service. If we serve without confession He wins. If we refuse to serve because of relational discord, He wins. The only way to disarm his plot is to confess and then serve with a clean heart. My kids have heard their daddy and me say so many times, "Family, if there's anything I've done that's out of line, please forgive me," that now we hear it coming from them at family prayer time.

Let God's Word evaluate your life for relational disharmony:

I Timothy 2:8 "Therefore I want the men in every place to pray, lifting up holy hands, without wrath and dissension." "You husbands likewise, live with your wives in an understanding way, as with a weaker vessel, since she is a woman; and grant her honor as a fellow heir of the grace of life, so that your prayers may not be hindered." I Peter 3:7

Forgive your brother from your heart (Matthew 1:35 NIV)

Dr. Neil Anderson says that forgiveness is agreeing to live with the consequences of another person's sin. Forgiveness is costly; we pay the price of the evil we forgive. Yet you're going to live with those consequences whether you want to or not; your only choice is whether you will do so in the bondage of bitterness or the freedom of forgiveness. That's how Jesus forgave you-He took the consequences of your sin upon Himself. All true forgiveness is substitutional, because no one really forgives without bearing the consequences of the other person's sin.

We are informed by the parable of the unforgiving servant that refusing to forgive results in a shortage of God's forgiveness towards us. We must daily remind ourselves of our multi-million dollar bill of sin stamped PAID IN FULL to find the motivation to do the same to the small change debtors in our lives.

Give us a heart ready to repent

As Ike and I have been used to help couples with marriage problems over the years, one thing has become clear. The most effective tool is a heart that is tender before the Lord in those who are seeking help. This is the one thing that can break down any walls of stubbornness and silence words of hurt. Without a heart that is softened before the Lord there is little hope for patching up a marital dispute. Defenses stay up and there is no real progress, just talk. That is why the condition of the heart is so important.

We must constantly be giving attention to the condition of our hearts. Any callousness towards the Lord, any hardening of our heart towards others will cut off His Lordship in an area of our lives.

Let God's Word create a tender heart in you:
"'Because your heart was tender and you humbled yourself before God, when you heard His words against this place and against its inhabitants, and because you humbled yourself before Me, tore your clothes, and wept before Me, I truly have heard you,' declares the Lord." II Chronicles 34:27 "O Lord, do not Thine eyes look for truth? Thou hast smitten them, But they did not weaken; Thou hast consumed them, but they refused to take correction. They have made their faces harder than rock; they have refused to repent." Jeremiah 5:3 "Perhaps they will listen and everyone will turn from his evil way, that I may repent of the calamity which I am planning to do to them because of the evil of their deeds." Jeremiah 26:3 "Those whom I love, I reprove and discipline; be zealous therefore, and repent." Revelation 3:19

— 7 —

Walking By The Spirit's Guidance Through Prayer

"The more that a man is joined up to Thee and the more that he is gathered together in Thee, the more he understandeth without labour high secret mysteries, for he hath received from above the light of understanding." Thomas 'A Kempis, <u>The Imitation of Christ</u>, p. 7.

I had been a Martha for many years in my service for the Lord. Hard work was the tool with which I was most acquainted. It wasn't until I began to see the power and potential of prayer that I realized the force and effectiveness it added to any Spirit-guided task. Projects used to begin with an evaluation of hours and manpower needed to bring about completion. Now projects are begun well before human effort even begins. The concept of an event, project or dream is begun on my knees. It is nurtured and watered on my knees and eventually the actual doing takes place.

Speaking engagements I accept begin with authorization from the Father. Then I ask for direction on a topic. He snags my thinking with a little phrase or passage from His Word and the adventure begins. Little details like what I will wear when I speak or what should be served at a meal I host are all things my Creator wants to have a part in. The more I ask for His will and desires, the more He offers inspiration and direction. I would never want to go back to the old way of doing ministry. It is harder and less effective. God knows how to aim my arrows and conserve my resources better than anyone else and He wants to show me how to do each thing "right."

"Moody testifies that never until he knew the fullness of the Spirit did he know the fullness of God's power in his preaching, but after that his preached words never failed of some fruitage." James McConkey, <u>The Three-Fold Secret of the Holy Spirit</u>, p. 1.

In preparing to speak at a women's retreat, I had prepared the messages during my quiet time over a period of many weeks and months, but as I drove to the actual location I began to fear that what I had prepared was not adequate. I reminded myself that each day I had sought the Lord and this was what He had given me to deliver. I reminded myself of God's promises to other speakers and went on with what I had planned to share. During the talk the Lord Himself did a bit of re-writing. Things I had planned to share were omitted and things I had not planned were inserted by the leading of the Holy Spirit. When the event was over I knew that I had experienced GRAIN (the work only God Himself can do). I decided I never again would be satisfied with STRAW (what I can do with my own human abilities). It amazed me to watch His work and to see the difference in quality He produced as compared to my own craftsmanship. Post speaking counseling with women who had attended the retreat revealed the Lord's wisdom in each thing He had allowed me to share. He had truly aimed my arrows.

I just finished reading through the book of Leviticus in my quiet time. It is not my favorite book of the Bible. I get lost in the endless lists and instructions, but Leviticus is an important part of the powerful Word of God for many reasons. First, it teaches us that God is concerned with the details of living. I used to think that God gave **only** ten commands, but as you read through this book, over and over you see that God commanded many things to Moses. Some of the things God commanded seem small in their importance to us, but ultimately they reflect the concern of our all wise Heavenly Father over the details of our lives.

I noted the many aspects of life that God gave commands for. For example, **He was concerned about their diet**. *He even told the Israelites that whenever they ate meat, the fat belonged to Him.* (If the Israelites obeyed God in this small detail they would live healthier as well as happier lives.) **He was concerned about how the poor would be provided for**. He told them not to glean the corners of the field, but to leave them as food for the poor and needy. (It is interesting that even those of humble means had to "work" for their supper.) **He personally arranged the order of the twelve tribes as they camped around the Tabernacle.** In so doing He also put them in order for marching into war. **He gave specific courses of action for bringing about justice** and for **protecting the land from abuse**. He instituted **national holidays**, which were "holy days" of rest, retreat and reflection. He set up **the "Sabbath" principle** which included a plan to release debtors from debt, a way to protect the inheritance of land allotments throughout generations, and the means to protect man from overwork: man's continual problem. God taught the sons of Israel about **handling diseases,**

community discipline and gave them **detailed instructions regarding worship** (its preparation and purpose). He hand-picked the sons of Aaron and their descendants for specific responsibilities connected with the Tabernacle. He even told them **how to pack everything as they moved** (which they did at His direction). Some of these instructions were for a specific purpose (moving across the wilderness), a limited time period (such as the period when worship occurred in the Tabernacle) and some are timeless principles put in place to forever protect God's people from their own weaknesses.

What a marvelous, caring God He is to be so concerned with details. So why is it when thinking of our own lives that we make so many decisions carelessly and dangerously on our own? One reason is that, in our own warped thinking, we don't want to "overload" God with too many things. So without much thinking or prayer, we head into situations and responsibilities He never intended for us to pursue, and then pray for His deliverance and resources to get us out of them. Imagine, over-estimating our own capacity for wisdom and at the same time under-estimating His!

I remember being taught as a child that the will of God was like the center of a bull's-eye and that there was a very "center" of God's will to be experienced. Then, while in college, I read a book that described God's will more as a giant playground. You could go anywhere you wanted as long as you stayed within the fence of His written will (i.e. the Ten Commandments, etc.) The latter was an interesting concept, but one I have since chosen to reject. I now believe, with all my heart, that every decision I am willing to bring before the Lord can result in a perfectly executed bull's-eye.

The whole key to this discussion is my willingness. Anything I am willing to seek the Lord's heart on, He is willing to help me with. He tells us in James that when we need wisdom and ask Him for it, the attitude of His heart is generosity, not stinginess. *James 1:5 "But if any of you lacks wisdom, let him ask of God, who gives to all men generously and without reproach, and it will be given to him."*

In our own family, this scripture has had very practical implications. When an opportunity comes up, such as the girls attending camp or participating in an after school activity, it immediately goes on our prayer list. In faith we tell the Lord, "You know what is best. Show us if this is really what you want our girls doing." Many times the Lord will answer back, "No." Sometimes I am disappointed by His answer, but I am never in doubt **that He has answered**. I know that my "limited thinking" can distort eternity's values and that only God's clear vision of all time can sort through the details. When God says, "Yes," there is real rejoicing, for we not only know that God has stamped this activity with **His approval**, but also with **His supply** and **His protection**.

Prayer Journal entries:

Summer 2002 - Can Beth go to camp? God answers, "Yes," by allowing her to sell nineteen cases of Sees candy.

Summer 2002 – Should Mary and Beth go to music camp at the school? God answers, "No," by not providing resources. We find a delight in sleeping in and spending time doing things together that wouldn't have been possible with a rigorous schedule of school. It's always easier to take a "no" when you are looking back in time.

8/10/02 Should I sign Beth up for a city-wide Christian drama program she's been begging to participate in? It costs money that God will have to provide. Will it be good for her? It's a challenge to get her to do all the things that need to be done each night: homework and music practice. Am I filling her schedule too full?

9/30/02 Beth gets a lead role in our own church's children's choir musical. I take this as God's answer. This will be demanding enough. I begin praying that God will help her with this part.

12/16/02 I watch the dress rehearsal of the musical. Even though I have been given indications that Beth is doing well on her lines, I see that there is much of the script she still has to memorize. We begin more concentrated work, but at the same time I remind the Lord that I have steadily trusted Him for His help.

12/18/02 The Lord helps Beth do a magnificent job on her part. Thank you Lord!

Calling My will God's will

This prayer process has also affected my own activities. When an opportunity used to come up I found that if it was something I didn't want to do, then I would tell the person asking that I would need to "pray about it." If, however, it was something I wanted to do, I would almost immediately say, "Yes!" This got me into trouble on more than one occasion. Now, however, I have begun taking every opportunity before the Lord. I have found that sometimes God's perfect will is something I would not normally choose to do on my own, and that sometimes His wonderful wisdom protects me from things that seem at first glance so good and pleasant to my eyes.

For example, there is a kids camp program that I have led several times. It is **HARD WORK** mainly because of the limited staff. One year I remember going to the Lord after they had called to see if I would teach. "Lord, you don't want me to do that again, do you?" That was pretty much the drift of my prayer. Yet week after week I felt the Lord asking me to trust Him for the strength, the content and the abilities needed to do this. I said, "Yes," to the call and strangely found that God began to give lessons, crafts and even at the last minute, a theme song. He brought every essential element, including a person to cut out one hundred wooden crafts, helpers, decorations and even the finances to cover materials. If I had made that decision on my own, I would have missed God's marvelous work, because I couldn't see "that far."

On the other hand, there have been times when something I loved to do was offered. One time I was salivating over the possibility of ministry involvement, but felt God over the days and weeks pressing me to say, "No." What ended up happening was that during the time period this activity would have happened, my father became seriously ill and needed my help. God knew about impending circumstances that I could have never foreseen.

I don't want to imply by these examples that what you want to do is never God's will and what you dislike IS His will. But, they are certainly not mandatory criteria for correct decision-making. If they were, Gideon would have never approached the Midianites with three hundred men armed with only trumpets and torches, and Abraham would have never left home without a map.

When we don't ask God for His 3-D wisdom or help, we find ourselves limited to our own mental resources and finite perspective. But when we lay our day timers, our check books and our hearts before Him, we discover that He is the God of details, the God of decisions, and the God who solves dilemmas.

There is one other major lesson that I appreciated through reading Leviticus. The phrase "just as the Lord had commanded Moses" appears fourteen times. If you add the times that phrase appears in Exodus (one time), Numbers (nineteen), Deuteronomy (five), and Joshua (seven) you can make the grand total of forty-six repetitions and see a pattern develop. Whenever Moses came to the Tent of Meeting and stood before the Lord, the Lord stated a plan that affected their personal, as well as national, lives. Whenever they obeyed His instructions, they experienced blessing, protection and resource. Marshall Foster, American historian and speaker, is correct in his statement that *covenant keepers always win and covenant breakers always lose.*

So keep this in mind the next time someone asks you to do refreshments for Little League, head up the Prison Visitation Ministry, or you simply get the urge to buy a new refrigerator. God has a plan and if you meet Him in the place of worship, and wait on Him, He'll gladly share it with you.

Prayer journal entry:

10/25/02 Should I continue to teach children on Wed. nights, or would you like me to teach adults? If you want a change Lord, you'll have to provide a volunteer to work with children.

11/10/02 Received a phone call from our children's director. It seems we have a new woman at our church that loves children's ministry and they were wondering if I'd like a break.

1/5/03 The new children's ministry program began, under Jeni's direction. God blessed them with 150% increase in attendance and an awesome program. I began teaching an adult class called *The Deeper Life* and experienced God's power and presence in that class also.

Maturity is seen through dependence on the Holy Spirit

The Apostle Paul was disappointed with the church at Corinth. It was because by now they should have known the difference between walking like men, which is following the natural directions of the flesh, and walking by the Spirit of God. Baby Christians are new at submitting their will to the Lordship of Christ, but when you have known Jesus for a long time, you should not still be choosing your own desires over God's wishes. It is an indication of their immature spiritual condition. They should have progressed past this logjam in development. They should have been hearing His voice through Scripture and the impressions of their heart. They should have allowed themselves to be led by the Spirit's guidance, but they are stuck in their childish, selfish ways.

Meditate on the difference Jesus wants us to see in this type of lifestyle choice: *"I gave you milk to drink, not solid food, for you were not yet able to receive it. Indeed, even now you are not yet able for you are still fleshly. For since there is jealousy and strife among you, are you not fleshly, and are **you not walking like mere men**?" I Corinthians 3:2-3 "You are looking at things as they **are outwardly**..." II Corinthians 10:7a "...who regard **us as if we walked according to the flesh**." II Corinthians 10:2b "But turning around and seeing His disciples, He rebuked Peter, and said, 'Get behind Me, Satan; for you are not setting your mind on God's interests, but man's.'" Mark 8:33 "Do you not know that you are a temple of God, and that <u>**the Spirit of God dwells in you**</u>? If any man destroys the temple of God, God will destroy him, for the temple of God is holy and **that is what you are**." I Corinthians 3:16-17 "For Christ also died for sins once for all, the just for the unjust, in order that He might bring us to God, having been put to death in the flesh, **but made alive in the spirit**." I Peter 3:1*

"God has called the Church of Christ to live in the power of the Holy Spirit, and the church is living for the most part in the power of human flesh and/or will and energy and effort apart from the Spirit of God." Andrew Murray, <u>Absolute Surrender</u>, p. 2

We must <u>internalize</u> the truth that God's Spirit is always present in our lives and that we can either follow His impulses or choose to ignore them. My friend, Linda Riley, discusses the notion of "anointed shopping" in <u>A Call to</u>

Love. She tells several stories of how the Holy Spirit, by speaking to her heart, helped her pick out perfect gifts for people, who were very blessed. As a result, I now ask for the Lord's help before I begin my Christmas shopping. I ask Him for his help when I am buying personal gifts. After the buying is done I ask Him to load in His power and love. I want God's gift to have its full impact. I have seen Him answer again and again.

Prayer journal entry:

9/19/02 Asked God to help me to do gift shopping today. Funds were limited and I had several gifts to purchase. He responded with great answers. One example: For a couple I love dearly who just had a child, God gave the suggestion of cutting out pop-up cards for unique baby stationary. (The card stock would cost about four dollars. I had a jar of unique buttons my mom had already given me. I had lots of different ribbon left over from other projects, and I already have lots of cute clip art on my computer.) They turned out so cute! I asked God to help me design them (He's the creator so I knew He'd have better ideas than I would). He responded with all kinds of color combinations, plus button and ribbon combinations that turned out to be stunning!

Sometimes people confuse "following the Spirit" with being spontaneous. This is not what I mean. I am not referring to following every whim that comes into our mind. (Satan can use this if we fail to "test the spirits.") I do very definitely mean to follow through on every strong (pounding) impression of the Holy Spirit. If you aren't sure, ask for confirmation. But don't get in the habit of asking God to confirm every little thing He asks you to do. When He needed someone to lay hands on Saul of Tarsus, He wanted a servant who would respond obediently. He found one in

Ananias. What would you do if God said, "Go over to Straight Street and lay your hands on a murderer today?"

I enjoyed reading Joy Dawson's book, **Forever Ruined for the Ordinary**, where she relates a miracle God did in helping them locate additional housing for Youth With a Mission students. In this instance God actually directed her husband, John, to turn the car this way and that until he came to an unfamiliar house. He went up to the door and explained to the occupant that because of overcrowding they had been looking for more student housing, and that God had directed him to this particular house. (You can read the whole story to see how they had already prayed and sought out conventional methods of locating available housing to no avail.) The owner of the house had been preparing it for another purpose, which had fallen through at the last minute. As a result, she was able to graciously make it available for their use, complete with food in the refrigerator, rent free for an entire year. God has never given me such detail oriented driving directions YET, but I pray that if He does, He will find me obedient in my response.

"I will instruct you and teach you in the way which you should go; I will counsel you with My eye upon you. Do not be as the horse or as the mule, which have no understanding, whose trappings include bit and bridle to hold them in check, otherwise they will not come near to you." Psalm 32:8,9

One Friday morning, after a prayer time at our church, I felt a strong impression to visit a young boy from our church that was a patient at UCLA Medical Center. Let me tell you right off that this did not seem to be a good idea to me. It was a Friday. There would be terrible traffic! It was a holiday weekend (Memorial Day) and the hospital was right where the worst traffic would be. I argued with the Lord, but knew that I would not have victory unless I obeyed. Pushing my human reasoning back to make room for the Spirit's leading, I headed down the road. Suddenly I had a thought, "Why not take my Mom and enjoy the ride together?" She was anxious to get out that day and as we got back onto the freeway I realized that without even thinking about it, the Lord had saved me time because now we could take the carpool lane. We drove straight there and although we weren't able to visit with his mom, we prayed for him and with his roommate. We even ran into another family who had a child there that we knew. We ate lunch, had a great time in each other's company, and returned in plenty of time to pick up my children from school.

On another occasion, the mother of my prayer partner was in a local rest home. I usually relied on the Lord's leading to visit her, and one day I had a strong impression to do so. It wasn't a convenient time and I wasn't too thrilled about it, but wanted to be obedient, so I went. As I prayed with Rachel, I became aware that her roommate was having difficulty breathing. I immediately asked her if she was saved and ready to meet Jesus. She replied that she was. We prayed and asked God for His comfort and perfect will. This seemed to help immediately. We got a nurse to adjust her oxygen and went on with our visit in the other part of the room. I found out later that her roommate had died that night. God's timing was crucial. He needed an obedient servant that day. One day's delay would have been too much.

I am not always obedient to the Lord. These parts are harder to put in a book than others. One day the Lord strongly impressed me to call a friend from church. But, it took three days for me to call her. Suddenly, as I was sitting in church listening to the Sunday morning sermon, I was moved to action. (The previous three days had been so hectic that although this need had made it onto my "to do" list, it hadn't been done.) I heard my husband say, "How can we expect God to bless us when we won't even do some little thing He has asked us to do?" That was all I needed to prompt me to slip out of church and make the phone call. Later that day, I got to pray intensely with the woman over a spiritual battle she had been fighting and within twenty-four hours we had seen an answer to that prayer that brought comfort for her anxious heart. Why do we wait when God tells us to do something?

If we study the life of Jesus Christ, we see that his actions, destinations and miracles were done through dependence on the Father and at the leading of the Spirit. (Co-dependency at its best.) This is what the great missionary statesman, Hudson Taylor, referred to as the "exchanged life."

Meditate on these examples of Spirit leading: *"Then Jesus was **led up by the Spirit** into the wilderness to be tempted by the devil." Matthew 4:1 "And immediately **the Spirit impelled Him to go out into the wilderness**. And He was in the wilderness **forty days being tempted by Satan**; and **He was with the wild beasts**, and the **angels were ministering to Him**." Mark 1:12-13 "And Jesus, **full of the Holy Spirit, returned from the Jordan and was led about by the Spirit in the wilderness.**" Luke 4:1 "And Jesus returned to Galilee **in the power of the Spirit**; and news about Him spread through all the surrounding district." Luke 4:14 "At that very time He **rejoiced greatly in the Holy Spirit**, and said, 'I praise Thee, O Father, Lord of heaven and earth, that Thou didst hide these things from the wise and intelligent and didst reveal them to babes. Yes, Father, for thus it was well-pleasing in Thy sight.' " Luke 10:21 "Until the day when He was taken up, after He had **by the Holy Spirit given orders** to the apostles whom He had chosen." Acts 1:2 "You know of Jesus of Nazareth, how **God anointed Him with the Holy Spirit and with power**, and how He went about doing good, and healing all who were oppressed by the devil; for God was with Him." Acts 10:38*

Prayer journal entry:

8/14/02 I asked the Lord to help us plan a tea for women from our church to be held in my home. We began asking for His presence and power. We asked for all the resources we would need.

8/24/02 In the middle of my quiet time, God gives the lesson I know should be used for the tea. I simply took "dictation" from His hand over the life of Deborah (I Samuel).

9/12/02 The tea went beautifully. The children played quietly as they enjoyed their own little picnic on the living room floor. The older children, who watched them, were loving and calm and they had fun. I had two *tea* angels offer to heat water. (Never having given a tea before, I hadn't anticipated this challenge.) The weather was perfect. And since the sliding glass door was opened at least fifty million times during the event, I was especially thankful that the flies didn't show up until the conclusion of the event.

Other godly people are listed as examples of Spirit walking. God wants us to know that it is an unseen, but tangible experience of direction.

Meditate on these examples from God's Word: *"And behold, there was a man in Jerusalem whose name was Simeon; and this man was righteous and devout, looking for the consolation of Israel; and the Holy Spirit was upon him. And it had been revealed to him by the Holy Spirit that he would not see death before he had seen the Lord's Christ. And he* **came in the Spirit into the temple***; and when the parents brought in the child Jesus, to carry out for Him the custom of the Law." Luke 2:25-27 "And the Spirit said to Philip, 'Go up and join this chariot.' " Acts 8:29 "And while Peter was reflecting on the vision,* **the Spirit said to him***, 'Behold, three men are looking for you.' " Acts 10:19 "And* **the Spirit told me**

to go with them without misgivings. And these six brethren also went with me, and we entered the man's house." Acts 11:12 *"And while they were ministering to the Lord and fasting, **the Holy Spirit said**, 'Set apart for Me Barnabas and Saul for the work to which I have called them.'"* Acts 13:2 *"So, **being sent out by the Holy Spirit**, they went down to Seleucia and from there they sailed to Cyprus."* Acts 13:4 *"But Saul, who was also known as Paul, **filled with the Holy Spirit**, fixed his gaze upon him."* Acts 13:9 *"And they passed through the Phrygian and Galatian region, **having been forbidden by the Holy Spirit to speak the word in Asia.**"* Acts 16:6 *"And when they had come to Mysia, they were trying to go into Bithynia, and **the Spirit of Jesus did not permit them**."* Acts 16:7 *"Now after these things were finished, Paul **purposed in the spirit** to go to Jerusalem after he had passed through Macedonia and Achaia, saying, 'After I have been there, I must also see Rome.'"* Acts 19:21

Paul is constantly trying to focus our attention on the leading (or baby-sitting role) of the Holy Spirit. *"**Live by the Spirit**, and you will not gratify the desires of the sinful nature."* Galatians 5:16 *"Now the Lord is the Spirit; and **where the Spirit of the Lord is, there is liberty.**"* II Corinthians 3:17 *"Who also made us adequate as servants of a new covenant, not of the letter, but of the Spirit; for the letter kills, **but the Spirit gives life**."* II Corinthians 3:6

"Abiding," is the most important principle to learn about Spirit directed teaching. Regular times of prayer and saturation in the Word are the means to counter the voice of our own flesh and that of the devil. The reason Jesus says that this "abiding" relationship is so crucial is that it is the means for God to prepare us for whatever situations we will face. If we abide we will bear fruit and our fruit will remain. If we abide we will pray the kinds of prayers that God answers.

Everything depends on this root to branch dependency.

Read what results from a connected relationship with God through prayer: *"Abide in Me, and I in you. As the branch cannot bear fruit of itself, unless it abides in the vine, so neither can you, unless you abide in Me. I am the vine, you are the branches; he who abides in Me, and I in him, he bears much fruit; for apart from Me you can do nothing." John 15:4-5 "Anyone who goes too far and does not abide in the teaching of Christ, does not have God; the one who abides in the teaching, he has both the Father and the Son." II John 1:9 "And as for you, the anointing which you received from Him abides in you, and you have no need for anyone to teach you; but as His anointing teaches you about all things, and is true and is not a lie, and just as it has taught you, you abide in Him." I John 2:27 "…remember that it is not you who supports the root, but the root supports you." Romans 11:18b*

Prayer journal entry:

9/25/02 After a special time of prayer at the church I felt an urge to go home. I had previously thought about going to Wal-mart to pick up some items for our mid-week kid's program. When I returned home, I found our house full of smoke. Earlier in the morning I had fried donuts for my kids. Because several appliances were plugged into one of those six-in-one outlets (I THOUGHT I had unplugged the correct cord), hot grease had been heating for over two hours and WOULD have caught our house on fire if I had gone to the store. Thank you Lord!

Wisdom is revealed through an intimate relationship with God

There is nothing that my Creator does not know. Therefore, when I see a lack of knowledge or wisdom, I need to seek more of Him. We are told that George Washington Carver's success with the peanut came about because every morning he said, "God, You made the peanut and You can tell me what it's good for." There is nothing about raising your kids, enhancing your marriage or being successful at your job, that God doesn't know. So, we should be encouraged to bring every little or big concern before His throne and receive the help we need in any area.

The Spirit shows us HOW to pray

My two girls will someday do great things for God. But right now their key responsibility is getting their mother to pray more. They do a great job of motivating me with their sibling rivalry. It seems they came out of the womb with a competitive streak asking, "Did my sister get anything so far that I didn't?" One day as I prayed for them the Holy Spirit used a passage in James to aim my prayers.

"But if you have bitter jealousy and selfish ambition in your heart, do not be arrogant and so lie against the truth. This wisdom is not that which comes down from above, but is earthly, natural, **demonic***. For where jealousy and selfish ambition exist, there is disorder and every evil thing. But the wisdom from above is first pure, then peaceable, gentle, reasonable, full of mercy and good fruits, unwavering, without hypocrisy. And the seed whose fruit is righteousness is sown in peace by those who make peace. What is the source of quarrels and conflicts among you? Is not the source your pleasures that wage war in your members? You lust and do*

not have; so you commit murder. And you are envious and cannot obtain; so you fight and quarrel. You do not have because you do not ask. You ask and do not receive, because you ask with wrong motives, so that you may spend it on your pleasures." James 3:14-4:3

God's Word helped direct my prayer at the root cause of their rivalry. There was jealousy and selfishness. That was obvious. But the idea that demons were at work to bring disorder to our lives was an eye-opening thought that day. If demons could cause turmoil in our lives, many others would be affected. In this passage, James points out that God's wisdom will be lived out in peace and gentleness, but that disorder is an earmark of "every evil thing." This helps us direct our prayers where they will do the most good. Communication, family prayer and maybe a spanking will help my children in the short run, but in-depth prayer aimed at the enemy and his tactic of introducing disorder, will gain the best advantage in the long run. I'm doing both. I don't want to take chances with their lives.

The Holy Spirit is our teacher

*"He shall glorify Me; for **He shall take of Mine, and shall disclose it to you**." John 16:14 "All things that the Father has are Mine; therefore I said, that **He takes of Mine, and will disclose it to you**." John 16:15 "But the Helper, the Holy Spirit, whom the Father will send in My name, **He will teach you all things, and bring to your remembrance all that I said to you**." John 14:26 "But when He, **the Spirit of truth, comes, He will guide you into all the truth; for He will not speak on His own initiative, but whatever He hears, He will speak; and He will disclose to you what is to come**." John 16:13 "It was revealed to them that they were not serving themselves, but you, in these things which now have been*

*announced to you through those **who preached the gospel to you by the Holy Spirit** sent from heaven— things into which angels long to look." I Peter 1:12*

Checking the root of impressions

Be suspicious of thoughts that would lead you away from your prayer and study time, but at the same time, be open to following thoughts that occur during your prayer and study time that lead you to action (writing a song, preparing a lesson, writing a spiritual letter, etc.). Jot things down for later that might make you miss the pearl of His presence.

8

Experiencing True Faith

"The lesson of faith once learned, is an everlasting acquisition and an eternal fortune made, and without trust even riches will leave us poor." Mrs. Charles Cowman, <u>Days of Heaven on Earth</u> *(Quoted in <u>Streams in the Desert</u>,) p. 2-3.*

Open God's Closet

One of the greatest lessons I have learned is that of opening God's closet. It happened that during a certain period of time our church received a number of charitable requests. A ministry to native Americans needed clothing. We responded by going home and cleaning out clothes from our closet. A prison ministry needed warm things for inmates in Mexico who were facing a cold winter. A ministry to the homeless in Los Angeles needed jackets. Again and again we went through the closet. It seemed that the requests kept coming and although my closet never became "empty," I suddenly realized that the need of the world was greater than the supply of my own personal closet. It was during this time that I re-read some of George Mueller's writings and came across the following quote:

"Often this last point has of late passed through my mind, and I have placed myself in the position of having no means at all left, and two thousand and one hundred persons not only daily at the table, but with everything else to be provided for, and all funds gone; 10 missionaries to be assisted, and nothing whatever left; about one hundred schools, with, about nine thousand scholars in them, to be entirely supported, and no means for them in hand; about four millions of tracts and tens of thousands of copies of the Holy Scriptures yearly now to be sent out, and all the money expended. Invariable, however, with this probability before me, I have said to myself, 'God, who has raised up this work through me, God who has led me generally year after year to enlarge it, God who has supported this work now for more than forty years, will still help, and will not suffer me to be confounded because I rely upon Him.'" George Mueller, <u>Answers to Prayer</u>, p.104-105

Consequently, I asked myself "Did George have more resources than I do?" The answer came back strongly, "No!" Then how was he able to have such an impact? How was he able to support missionaries, run schools, care for orphans, distribute Bibles and tracts and all without a penny in his pocket? The answer was that George was rich in a commodity I needed more of: faith. George simply believed God for more. It was as if he had learned to open a door that led beyond his own limited means into God's well-provisioned walk-in closet. This truth encouraged me to ask for things beyond the limits of my own supply.

When you understand this truth there will be no limits to what you can ask for. Normally our mind plays tricks by convincing us that some things are just "not possible." Once this roof over your prayers is removed you will find a galaxy of possibilities for God to work through.

Prayer journal entry:

7/6/01 Ike and I attended the banquet for the anti-abortion youth ministry SURVIVORS and heard their plea for funds to make a video. Asked God to "open up His closet" for them.
9/14/02 Prayed at the abortion clinic with the SURVIVORS. Found out from their leader that shortly after the banquet ALL the funds had come in to pay for the movie. Thank you Lord.

"True faith drops its letter in the post office box, and lets it go. Distrust holds on to a corner of it, and wonders that the answer never comes." Mrs. Charles Cowman, <u>Days of Heaven upon Earth.</u>

Prayer journal entry:

8/3/01 I asked God to open up ten thousand dollars for our church/school library. (I had seen its effectiveness in reaching families with books and videos. I could envision a place called "The Room of the Book" totally devoted to the study of God's Word with resources, computer programs, etc.)
11/24/01 We received gifts of two thousand dollars (Because funds were short at school this money had to be used for librarian's salaries instead of the development of an additional adult facility. This was divine provision, though, because without these funds the library would have been forced to close its doors for an extended period of time.)
10/27/02 I asked the Lord for direction on whether or not this library idea was lining up with His will and purposes.

12/6/02 A gift of one thousand dollars is given.

12/18/02 A gift of another thousand dollars is given. (The librarian is committed to expanding our current library to two rooms.)

2/4/03 The librarian informs the group who prays on Tuesday morning that she feels the "go ahead" from God to begin getting the shelves built. She asks for us to pray that the Lord will help in the process.

"Faith is to believe what we do not see, and the reward of this faith is to see what we believe." Saint Augustine

Prayer journal entry:

12/30/01 As we ministered to the elderly residents at Crown Pointe Retirement Home I breathed a prayer that we could someday have a van or bus to pick up residents and bring them to church and other events. Their bus driver does not drive on Sundays.

1/2/03 Word came that our church would be given an eighteen-passenger mini bus for free.

2/4/03 The bus arrives. It is beautiful. We are also to receive a 45-passenger bus for free soon. God is good!

Faith is taking God at His Word

*"And after they had hoisted it up, they used supporting cables in undergirding the ship; and fearing that they might run aground on the shallows of Syrtis, they let down the sea anchor, and so let themselves be driven along. The next day as we were being violently storm-tossed, they began to jettison the cargo; and on the third day they threw the ship's tackle overboard with their own hands. And since neither sun nor stars appeared for many days, and no small storm was assailing us, from then on **all hope of our***

being saved was gradually abandoned*. And when they had gone a long time without food, then Paul stood up in their midst and said, 'Men, you ought to have followed my advice and not to have set sail from Crete, and incurred this damage and loss. And yet now I urge you **to keep up your courage**, for there shall be no loss of life among you, but only of the ship. Therefore, **keep up your courage, men,** for I believe God **that it will turn out exactly as I have been told**.' " Acts 27:17-22, 25*

In this Scripture, we read of an incident in the life of Paul in which his circumstances are screaming, "No hope." Yet his hope is not robbed along with that of the men he travels with. His hope is secure because it rests on the Word of God, which is unable to be false. He has been in a storm for two weeks. There is no sign of sun or stars. What a storm this must have been! But Paul, who has been informed by an angel that he will stand before Caesar, believes God. This is the essence of true faith, and we will find it an essential ingredient if our prayers are to be birthed in the miraculous: We must trust God's Word, in the midst of the storm, that God's promises will turn out **exactly as we have been told**.

"Or has He spoken, and will He not make it good?" Numbers 23:19 "So faith comes from hearing, and hearing by the word of Christ." Romans 10:17

Prayer journal entry:

10/6/02 After a conversation with a friend, Sheryl, who felt God had pricked her heart to hold a silent auction for scholarship money for needy students at our school, I asked God to help us.

11/09/02 While ministering at a women's retreat, held in

the Costa Mesa Hilton Hotel, I wandered downstairs and discovered the silent auction of a huge Catholic school. The people running this auction had perfected the art of fundraising. They gave me a copy of their catalog, complete with names and addresses of sponsoring businesses. We also got limits lifted off our own perceptions as we gained new ideas of HOW we could raise more money for students who needed help.

02/04/03 There are many donations being received for the auction and a sense of God's hand in the details.

02/25/03 Sheryl is working hard to complete God's mission. I am praying for physical strength for her. We raised $7,100.

"'For My hand made all these things, thus all these things came into being,' declares the Lord. 'But to this one I will look, to him who is humble and contrite of spirit, and who trembles at My word.'" Isaiah 66:2

True faith is the essence of spiritual experience

You cannot come to God without faith. You cannot be justified without it. You cannot know God without it. You cannot be healed without it. You cannot please God without it. You cannot make progress in your relationship with God without it. You cannot see God without it. You cannot experience the blessing of God without it. You cannot fight an invisible enemy without it. It is the absolute essential of a living, vibrant walk with God. Therefore faith greatly deserves our attention. You can find a detailed Scriptural study to use in your prayer time that supports this idea at our website: www.oliveleafpublications.com.

For example, each of my daughters recently had a friend over to play. After a long day, we began to get ready to take them home and get ready for church that night. One of the girls asked it she could go too. I began making all kinds of excuses: "I have to be there so early for rehearsal and I have so much to do to get ready to lead the children's program..." She looked disappointed and I could visualize the Lord looking in a similar way. A few minutes later I called her downstairs and told her that the Lord had softened my heart and that she could go to church with us. The first words out of her mouth were "Can I spend the night too?" The thought flashed through my mind that I want to have that kind of faith in my praying. I want to press God for all that He is willing to do.

I have a cat named Charlie. Often, when he hears me turn over in the night, he will move quietly on the bed near my hand. I will, many times, reach out my hand into the darkness, feel for his smooth back and begin to stroke his soft fur. But there are times I am too tired. I lay my hand back down. It's then that Charlie gently nudges me with his nose. It is a firm, but gentle nudge. To tell you the truth, Charlie can get me to pet him much longer than I would without his nudging. He keeps sticking his nose under my hand and I keep responding. This is how our faith prompts God to do His great works. Our faith just nestles into His will and Word and his hand responds with action.

Prayer journal entry:

9/22/02 I asked the Lord if we could somehow have the resources to give the residents at Crown Pointe Retirement Home a Christmas gift.

12/22/02 We were able through generous hearts to give fifty gift baskets to the residents who attend the Hymn Night service our church provides. Each basket contained a CD or cassette of hymns sung by my friend Cal, baked goodies, an angel pin, and a little pop-up book with a record of miracles God has done for our church. Isn't God good?

Prayer journal entry:

10/1/02 A group of women from our church were planning on visiting a ministry to unwed mothers run by our friends, Dr. Al and Judy Howard. The ministry is called His Nesting Place and it houses women who decide to keep their babies rather than abort them. I asked God to help us take resources that would bless them. I didn't have much money to buy baby clothes or equipment myself. I would have to trust God for what they needed. We put a bulletin announcement in about the trip and a request for items.

11/06/02 I found out from my husband that our church had included this ministry in our yearly missions budget for the coming year. What a blessing that knowledge was.

11/07/02 The day of the trip we loaded a complete van and trunk with beautiful, barely used, cribs, clothing and other baby necessities. The Lord answered this prayer with abundance.

"Do not throw away your confidence; it will be richly rewarded. You need to persevere so that when you have done the will of God, you will receive what he has promised." Hebrews 10:35-36 NIV

Evil and unbelief go together in God's evaluation

When the children of Israel doubt God's ability to care for them, He gets angry. He delivers dinner to them and while they are eating it His anger strikes. Many die as a result of their distrust. Later, at the edge of the Promised Land, they have another opportunity to trust Him. Their board meeting ends in a ten to two defeat for God's plan. Again, many die as a result of distrust. In the New Testament book of Hebrews, God speaks about their failure to trust Him. Hebrews 3:8-12

"Do not harden your hearts as when they provoked Me, as in the day of trial in the wilderness, where your fathers tried Me by testing Me, and saw My works for forty years. Therefore I was angry with this generation, and said, 'They always go astray in their heart; and they did not know My ways, as I swore in My wrath, they shall not enter My rest.' Take care, brethren, lest there should be in any one of you an evil, unbelieving heart, in falling away from the living God." God is thoroughly astonished that His people could watch Him work for forty years and still not get it. How could they not know He was faithful? Had they not drunk water from a rock? Had they not picked up tasty meals each day off the desert floor? Had they not seen their shoes not wear out on the hot sand? Had they somehow missed His guiding presence in the sky every day and night?

Can you relate? What have you seen God do over the last forty years? Have you seen His faithful character? Has He cared for you, protected you and guided you? Do you still not get it? Nothing pushes God's button faster than distrust. He doesn't mince words about it. He frames disbelief right along with evil.

"And Jesus, aware of this, said to them, 'Why do you discuss the fact that you have no bread? Do you not yet see or understand? Do you have a hardened heart? Having eyes, do you not see? And having ears, do you not hear? And do you not remember, when I broke the five loaves for the five thousand, how many baskets full of broken pieces you picked up?' They said to Him, 'Twelve.' 'And when I broke the seven for the four thousand, how many large baskets full of broken pieces did you pick up?' And they said to Him, 'Seven.' And He was saying to them, 'Do you not yet understand?'" Mark 8:17-21 *"For they had not gained any insight from the incident of the loaves, but their heart was hardened."* Mark 6:52

True faith is God's love language

Those of us in the Christian community have learned, thanks to authors like Gary Smalley, that there are five different love languages that express love to different types of people. Some feel loved best by acts of service, others prefer gifts, touch, notes or time. But there is no better way to say, "I love you," to God than through our "belief" in Him and in His ability to handle the things that come our way.

When I served as a children's pastor, in Orange County, California, I purchased a tiny, baby bunny to help the children learn their memory verses. (It was Easter time and "Pinky" served double duty in the petting zoo.) The children could take Pinky home for three or four days after they had said three memory verses. This worked out perfectly, because it meant I only had to deal with him on Sundays and Wednesdays. At first, Pinky produced a flurry of activity. Kids were fighting to see who could say their verses first and claim the privilege of taking Pinky home. He was adorable. He was so little and cute. But as Pinky began to grow, lugging him home and cleaning out his cage became less and less popular. More and more Pinky hung out at the children's building with me. I knew he needed exercise, so everyday I would let him run around in the little grassy area where the swings were located. He often disappeared from sight, but when it was time for me to go home I would put a carrot in his cage and sure enough, soon he would be nibbling away. This routine went on for months before tragedy struck. One night I went out as usual to get Pinky tucked away for the night. I put in the carrot, but Pinky never appeared. When I shared his disappearance with the kids at church, they did two things: they looked everywhere for him AND they began to pray. Every SS class, every choir rehearsal, every mid-week program's prayer time began with the sound of little children pleading for God to bring back Pinky. I hate to admit it, but this was one of the times in my life when my faith was flat. I had no hope that Pinky would ever be found. But that's the great thing about faith. God says He just looks for a mustard seed of it. The smallest bit is powerful enough to bring about a miracle. As sure as you are reading this right now, about a year after Pinky disappeared I heard a knock on my office door. There were two neighborhood boys with a humongous white rabbit, complete with Pinky's markings and a lot of dirt. They had found him in a field across the street from the church. How glad I was that my faith-less-ness had not infected the children. Instead, their faith taught mine a lesson.

When our church was small another friend of mine shared an infectious faith. Up to that point we had relied on a little six channel mixer for our sound and it had literally given its life for our services. A new one had to be purchased and our soundman had located a great deal. We could buy a huge, good quality mixer that normally sold for nine thousand dollars for only four thousand eight hundred dollars. I remember as he presented this passionate dream to our little congregation of about seventy. It doesn't seem like that much money now, but back then it seemed as plausible as a trip to the moon. Sometimes I think God performs miracles just to illustrate our smallmindedness and this was one of those times. Within two weeks all the money had been given and that mixer is still in use in our youth facility. I felt so foolish for not trusting God.

Make God Marvel at Your Faith

I love the story of the centurion who made Jesus marvel by His faith (Matthew 8). He comes in the midst of tragedy. His beloved servant is dying. This was the 911 call of its day. Yet he tells Jesus that there is no need to go to his servant. "Just speak the word" is his request. That is what I desire more than anything in my walk with Him. I want to make Him gasp by the hope I have in His Word.

True faith kicks out doubt

Faith and doubt cannot be roommates and so in order for you to trust God, you will have to kick doubt out. They can't survive in the same house so you'll have to choose between them. They are totally incompatible by nature. They cannot co-exist. You must let one move in and see the other to the door.

"And immediately Jesus stretched out His hand and took hold of him, and said to him, 'O you of little faith, why did you doubt?'" Matthew 14:31

"And Jesus answered and said to them, 'Truly I say to you, if you have faith, and do not doubt, you shall not only do what was done to the fig tree, but even if you say to this mountain, "Be taken up and cast into the sea," it shall happen.'" Matthew 21:21

True faith overrides intellect

Many times God works through the brain He gave us to help us know Him better. But there are times when we have to believe even beyond what we can understand. I cannot explain the complexities of DNA, but I can believe the One who thought it up. I cannot come up with an explanation of how anyone could create our universe in six days, but I know the One who did it. So my faith has to leap beyond what I can understand or explain.

"...that your faith should not rest on the wisdom of men, but on the power of God." I Corinthians 2:5

"Where is the wise man? Where is the scribe? Where is the debater of this age? Has not God made foolish the wisdom of the world? For since in the wisdom of God the world through its wisdom did not come to know God, God was well-pleased through the foolishness of the message preached to save those who believe." I Corinthians 1:20-21

True faith is seen in how we strike

"And Elisha said to him, 'Take a bow and arrows.' So he took a bow and arrows. Then he said to the king of Israel, 'Put your hand on the bow.' And he put his hand on it, then **Elisha laid his hands on the king's hands**. *And he said, 'Open the window toward the east,' and he opened it. Then Elisha said,* **'Shoot!'** *And he shot. And he said,* **'The Lord's arrow of victory, even the arrow of victory over Aram**; *for you shall defeat the Arameans at Aphek until you have destroyed them.' Then he said, 'Take the arrows,' and he took them. And he said to the king of Israel,* **'Strike the ground,' and he struck it three times and stopped**. *So the man of God was angry with him and said, 'You should have struck five or six times, then you would have struck Aram until you would have destroyed it. But now you shall strike Aram only three times.' " II Kings 13:15-19*

This is an interesting passage of Scripture. King Joash tells Elisha that this arrow represents victory over an ungodly enemy and then he is told to strike the ground with it. We see the puny quality of his faith as he only strikes three times. If I handed you an arrow, and told you that this arrow represented help for abused children, change for alcoholic lives, hope for world hunger, and then told you to strike the ground, how many times would you strike? We don't know a lot about the king, but we know this much: he could only trust God for a little.

"The beginning of anxiety is the end of faith, and the beginning of true faith is the end of anxiety." George Mueller

Prayer journal entry:

1/19/02 My friend asks prayer for a financial situation that has put them in a bind. I am concerned for their family, but I don't have the resources to help. I must tap into God's resources to make a difference.

1/26/02 I find out that the Lord took care of the whole situation.

Use these truths to show fear to the door: *Philippians 4:6-7 "Be anxious for nothing, but in everything by prayer and supplication with thanksgiving let your requests be made known to God. And the peace of God, which surpasses all comprehension, shall guard your hearts and your minds in Christ Jesus." Psalm 34:4 "I sought the Lord, and He answered me, and delivered me from all my fears." Psalm 56:3 "When I am afraid, I will put my trust in Thee." Isaiah 12:2 "Behold, God is my salvation, I will trust and not be afraid; for the Lord God is my strength and song, and He has become my salvation."*

True faith kicks out sight

In planning a tea we called on 15 hostesses to decorate tables. This would provide sufficient seating for all the women who had signed up, plus a few extra seats. Some of the women came the night before to set up. What beautiful themes their tables displayed. Gleaming crystal and china, fresh flowers, linen napkins and more would make each woman feel special as she came to have her heart refreshed through fellowship and the Word. The morning of the event we still had four tables that hadn't been decorated. Imagine our dismay when five women showed up with decorations. We soon discovered that we had made a mistake and wouldn't need the last woman to decorate after all. Sandy was visibly disappointed, but let it go and put her decorations back in the car. We had prayed so diligently that God would oversee the details of this morning. It seemed hard to understand. After most of the women had found their seats we still had guests arriving. Amazingly enough we had eight extra women show up. To pull out paper plates just wouldn't have cut it that day. Smiling, our "extra" hostess quickly pulled out eight china plates and set a beautiful table. God had seen to the details!

"Abraham believed God and said to sight, 'stand back!' and to the laws of nature, 'Hold your peace!' and to a misgiving heart, 'Silence, thou lying temptor!' He believed God." Joseph Parker (Quoted by Mrs. Charles Cowman, <u>Streams in the Desert</u>, p. 12)

"The other disciples therefore were saying to him, 'We have seen the Lord!' But he said to them, 'Unless I shall see in His hands the imprint of the nails, and put my finger into the place of the nails, and put my hand into His side, I will not believe.' Jesus said to him, 'Because you have seen Me, have you believed? Blessed are they who did not see, and yet believed.'" John 20:25, 29

<u>Prayer journal entry:</u>

11/15/02 On Friday evening, I suddenly discover that my oven will not work. I have a huge group of people coming over for dinner on Sunday. There is not enough time to call a repair man because Saturday is already filled with ministry commitments. We try everything to get it to work, but go to bed with no encouragement.

11/16/02 I ask God to PLEASE make my oven work. Later on in the day I try to turn it on and **it works**.

11/17/02 I am able to serve the meal.

12/3/02 My oven goes out again. There is time to call the repair man.

12/09/02 My oven gets fixed for a third of the estimated price because my husband does price checking and confronts the company's high appraisal.

"Jesus therefore said to him, 'Unless you people see signs and wonders, you simply will not believe.'" John 4:4

True faith blows the limitations off of godly dreams

"Now to Him who is able to do exceeding abundantly beyond all that we ask or think, according to the power that works within us." Ephesians 3:20 "Truly, truly, I say to you, he who believes in Me, the works that I do shall he do also; and greater works than these shall he do; because I go to the Father." John 14:12 "Jesus answered and said to him, 'Because I said to you that I saw you under the fig tree, do you believe? You shall see greater things than these.'" John 1:50 "And He said to them, 'Because of the littleness of your faith; for truly I say to you, if you have faith as a mustard seed, you shall say to this mountain, "Move from here to there," and it shall move; and nothing shall be impossible to you.'" Matthew 17:20

The night I first met my husband he began to lay out the dreams God had given him for Olive Branch. "We will have a home for unwed mothers, a place where retired Christian workers can live reasonably, schooling through college..." He went on and on describing all his wonderful dreams for ministries. My thoughts were stuck in the immediate. "Don't you think you better start small? Didn't you say that your church doesn't even have a copy machine?" Years later as I see others catch the vision for those dreams I am sorry that sometimes I am content with "copy machine" dreams.

When my husband has read a great book and is touched by it, many times he will pick up the phone and try to procure the author to speak to our church. This has always seemed outrageous to me. We don't offer big honorariums. Our small congregation could not have expected to obtain the services of such nationally recognized speakers. But thanks to this bold dreamer, our congregation has enjoyed some of the best teaching in the country.

True faith kicks out familiar expectations

"And He went out from there, and He came into His home town; and His disciples followed Him. And when the Sabbath had come, He began to teach in the synagogue; and the many listeners were astonished, saying, 'Where did this man get these things, and what is this wisdom given to Him, and such miracles as these performed by His hands? Is not this the carpenter, the son of Mary, and brother of James, and Joses, and Judas, and Simon? Are not His sisters here with us?' And they took offense at Him. And Jesus said to them, 'A prophet is not without honor except in his home town and among his own relatives and in his own household.' And He could do no miracle there except that He laid His hands upon a few sick people and healed them. And He wondered at their unbelief." Mark 6:1-6a

Location is everything. In this passage they were in Jesus' hometown. **We know that sometimes the familiar is a barrier to faith**. How often do we fail to even ask the Lord about a situation where someone has suffered for a long time? We have become more comfortable with the familiar than we are with faith. How many times had the disciples passed the pool called Bethesda and never given a thought to seeing the lame man healed? He had sat there for thirty-eight years. Who is near you, stuck in illness or a rotten marriage, that you have failed to pray for just because their situation has *always* been that way?

Have you ever experienced others limiting your potential by their lack of confidence? You might be quite proficient at something, but others, because they have not "seen you in action," doubt your ability. They do not receive the benefit of your ability because they do not believe you can do it. This is how God feels when we don't even lift our heads to trust Him.

This is exactly what happened when Jesus returned to His hometown and could only do a few miracles there. After all, as far as the townspeople were concerned, carpenters couldn't do miracles. Our limited perspective hinders future opportunities. We limit others and ourselves from answers to prayer because "we've never seen it done that way before."

"If they had been asked whether God could provide streams in the desert, they would have answered, yes. God had done it; He could do it again. But when the thought came of God doing something new, they limited Him. Their expectation could not rise beyond their past experience or their own thoughts of what was possible. Even so we may be limiting God by our conceptions of what He has promised or is able to do. Do let us beware of limiting the Holy One of Israel in our very prayer." Andrew Murray, <u>Waiting on God</u>, *p. 69.*

Faith is seen in ASKING

"Now a certain woman of the wives of the sons of the prophets cried out to Elisha, 'Your servant my husband is dead, and you know that your servant feared the Lord; and the creditor has come to take my two children to be his

slaves.' And Elisha said to her, 'What shall I do for you? Tell me, what do you have in the house?' And she said, 'Your maidservant has nothing in the house except a jar of oil.' Then he said, 'Go, borrow vessels at large for yourself from all your neighbors, even empty vessels; do not get a few. And you shall go in and shut the door behind you and your sons, and pour out into all these vessels; and you shall set aside what is full.' So she went from him and shut the door behind her and her sons; they were bringing the vessels to her and she poured. And it came about when the vessels were full, that she said to her son, 'Bring me another vessel.' And he said to her, 'There is not one vessel more.' And the oil stopped. Then she came and told the man of God. And he said, 'Go, sell the oil and pay your debt, and you and your sons can live on the rest.'" II Kings 4:1-7

In this passage the widow appears to have internalized the truth of Hebrews 11:6 even though it hasn't been written yet. (*And without faith it is impossible to please Him, for he who comes to God must believe that He is, and that He is a rewarder of those who seek Him.*) Most of us believe that God exists. It's the second part of the sentence we struggle with. Does He really reward? Would this be a time to count on that character quality? Would we be overstepping our bounds by leaning on Him and expecting something from Him? We spend more time asking questions of ourselves than we do asking for help from the one who can provide the answer. The widow's obedience is refreshing, she asks.

Our little widow woman comes to Elisha confident of two things: her husband feared the Lord and the creditors are about to make her sons slaves to pay for their debts. As her husband was a godly man she realizes that there is some incongruity between the promises of God and her situation. Her hubby feared God and now God is not making good on His promise to care for her and her son.

Prayer journal entry:

9/00 We begin praying for one of our teachers who has a car situation. Her car keeps breaking down and it is using up valuable energy.

12/00 She receives a gift of four hundred dollars that helps her make some needed repairs.

8/02 She is given the gift of a brand new car. Praise the Lord!

There is a myriad of promises for those who truly fear the Lord where provision is concerned. Here are just a few: *"Then it shall come about, because you listen to these judgments and keep and do them, that the Lord your God will keep with you His covenant and His lovingkindness which He swore to your forefathers. And He will love you and bless you and multiply you; He will **also bless the fruit of your womb and the fruit of your ground, your grain and your new wine and your oil**, the increase of your herd and the young of your flock, in the land which He swore to your forefathers to give you."* Deuteronomy 7:12-13 *"Behold, the eye of the Lord is on those who fear Him, on those who hope for His lovingkindness."* Psalm 33:1 *"O fear the Lord, you His saints; for to those who fear Him, there is no want."* Psalm. 34:9 *"But seek first His kingdom and His righteousness; **and all these things shall be added to you**."* Matthew 6:33 *"And my God shall supply **all your needs** according to His riches in glory in Christ Jesus."* Philippians 4:19

Our little widow woman is confused by the apparent lack of fulfillment of the principles noted above. She is asking the Lord, through His representative, to complete what is lacking in the covenant relationship. She is a witness that her husband completed his part of the bargain. Who knows better than a wife does if a husband truly feared the Lord or performed lip service instead?

Have you ever stood at the **Crossroads of Contradiction**? God's Word says, "thus and so," about how life should be, and YOUR reality says something altogether different? Faith is what causes you to look up and say, "God, you are the only one that can make *my physical reality match the spiritual reality you intended.*" Faithful praying braids the two together.

Faith asks, reminds, and sometimes even cries out for the things that are needed. This is why the picture of another widow woman (the one in the New Testament) is so profound. This widow realizes that she has NO OPTIONS. She is the picture of helplessness. Without intervention she is doomed. So she comes every day to ask. She bothers the judge so much that he gives in. Faith is the fuel that gets her to the judges' door each day. Without faith, she would have stayed in bed and missed God's best.

It's not just faith that is needed in such circumstances, but faith in the right source. Without faith IN GOD she would have been content to handle the situation with her own worldly plans. She might have asked for a job or a loan. But her faith in the Lord is seen in her persistent request for help. She's been promised that the children of the righteous shouldn't be out begging for bread and she wants to live it... so she asks.

*"Behold, as for the proud one, His soul is not right within him; but the righteous **will live by his faith**." Habakkuk 2:4*

Have you ever been sustained by faith? Has your daily existence been totally dependent on the provision of God? Those who have, know that it's FAITH in a God of faithfulness that is the daily bread you live on until your stomach, as well as your heart is full. Ask John the Baptist, who had no ATM or credit card, to give him locusts and honey. "How does

God provide for a prophet of the Lord?" Or ask Elijah who sat waiting for dinner to be brought, not by the pizza delivery boy, but by ravens who had been commanded by God. Either, all the promises of God are true, or they are all false. Either He can sustain life, or He can't. But puny things like circumstances cannot limit him if He truly is the God of the universe.

I experienced this in my own circumstances when someone stole my husband's identity. A man got Ike's Social Security number and began living high on the hog. (But it was our hog he was eating.) In trying to stop his efforts, we cancelled the overdraft protection on our checking account. After contacting every utility and credit card company, we eventually got all his transactions cleared off our credit report. But in the midst of the turmoil we experienced an interesting trial.

One Friday afternoon, the girls and I stopped to get some cash on our way to get an ice cream cone and a car wash. I was shocked, when for the first time in my life, the ATM wouldn't give me any money. I tried to explain to the machine that we were in the middle of "identity theft" and that we had temporarily unlinked the overdraft protection on our account, but it just blinked back with a stern response: "no money for you." I turned to the kids and said, "Well, if God wants us to have a car wash and an ice cream, He'll have to provide it." (God was listening to my conversation.)

The next day I went with friends to lead worship as a guest musician for a local church's women's event. When the day was over they thanked us with some unforgettable gifts. First, we each got a tube of mascara. (My friend Jim, who played guitar that day, really appreciated that one.) There were some little boxes of chocolate and some leftover door prizes in a bag given to our group. I let everyone else pick their gift and when they were done I looked inside the bag. Guess what was left. It was a free car wash coupon. But that wasn't all that happened on this adventure with God.

That night my husband and I were treated to a beautiful dinner by the elders of our church in honor of Pastor Appreciation Month. At the dinner, they presented us with different gift certificates. Among them were several for Baskin Robbins Ice Cream. Isn't God great? He wants Elijah, to know that He can meet every need. He wants us to know it as well.

Many times I have tested God's Word to us, such as where He promises that He can dress us better than the lilies of the field (Matthew 6). Our family has long been blessed with hand-me-downs from others in our church, and the timing of these gifts is never a coincidence.

One time I was preparing to speak at a convention and thought I needed something new and spiffy for the occasion. In my quiet time, I had reminded God of His promise to dress me better than Solomon's glory, and was not surprised when the same day my mother gave me a check for fifty dollars. But later in the day God clearly told me that the fifty dollars was NOT for my new clothing. It was to provide free resources for the people to whom I would be speaking. With it, CDs could be purchased and that meant that every participant would be saved hundreds of hours in file preparation. I am glad to say that this was one of those times I obeyed the Lord. In response to that obedience, the Lord prompted a friend to give me a little note the next day. When I opened it, the note read, "The Lord told me to give this to you." Inside was a gift certificate to a clothing store for fifty dollars. As it turned out, the store was having a big clearance sale and I got much more than fifty dollars worth of clothes out of the deal. Thank you Lord for being true to your Word!

God's Word tells us what we can ask for

It is a result of our limited thinking that we aim to pursue prayer to the neglect of reading God's Word, and that we attempt to become wiser in God's Word with a limited offering of prayer. You see these two are interdependent. Prayer opens up that which we don't understand about the Word. The Word opens up that which we don't understand about prayer. To grow in prayer we must grow in our ability to "wield the Word." *Jeremiah 33:3 says "Call to Me, and I will answer you, and I will tell you great and mighty things, which you do not know."* Prayer is the can opener that releases the things that are hard for us to understand about God's Word. When we are in an honest relationship with our Father, He promises in Prov. 1:23 to help us understand His Words. *"Turn to my reproof, Behold, I will pour out my spirit on you; I will make my words known to you."* In the same way, God's Word is a training manual for prayer.

If we don't know the Word, we can pass up His benefits

An ignorance of God's Word is like an ignorance of the current tax laws. Not only can you end up severely penalized for many years, but you can also deprive yourself of many benefits and credits that are legally yours and easily available. Hosea 4:6 tells us we are "destroyed for lack of knowledge." We reject true knowledge when we forget the law of our God. Even those who we would identify as appearing to be "wise" cannot have real wisdom if they have rejected the Bible, the living, active Word of God as total truth.

Prayer journal entry:

8/6/01 Ike needs new tires. We don't see the resources to pay for them right now.

8/26/01 I lead worship at a retreat and make a joke in passing about my calling to pray and that I can't seem to find a job that will pay me to do it.

8/27/01 God is down right angry with me for joking

about His provision. I am ashamed of how I have treated Him when He has been so good to me. I apologize to the man with whom I joked.

8/27/01 My honorarium, which is much more than I anticipated, is exactly enough to pay for four new tires.

Give your faith a workout with God's Word:

"But if God so arrays the grass of the field, which is alive today and tomorrow is thrown into the furnace, will He not much more do so for you, O men of little faith?" Matthew 6:30 *"You did not choose Me, but I chose you, and appointed you, that you should go and bear fruit, and that your fruit should remain,* **that whatever you ask of the Father in My name, He may give to you.**" John 15:16 *"And in that day you will ask Me no question. Truly, truly, I say to you,* **if you shall ask the Father for anything, He will give it to you in My name**." John 16:23 *"Until now you have asked for nothing in My name;* **ask, and you will receive, that your joy may be made full.**" John 16:24

Faith is seen in ACTION

"We must learn to take God at His Word, and go straight on in duty, although we see no way in which we can go forward. The reason we are so often balked by difficulties is that we expect to see them removed before we try to pass through them." Mrs. Charles Cowman, <u>Evening Thoughts</u>, (Quoted in <u>Streams in the Desert</u>, p. 55.)

It isn't faith that doesn't take a step

"And it shall come about when the soles of the feet of the priests who carry the ark of the Lord, the Lord of all the

*earth, shall rest in the waters of the Jordan, the waters of the Jordan shall be cut off, and the waters which are flowing down from above shall stand in one heap." Joshua 3:13 "And when He saw them, He said to them, 'Go and show yourselves to the priests.' And it came about that **as they were going**, they were cleansed." Luke 17:14 "Jesus said to him, 'Go your way; your son lives.' The man believed the word that Jesus spoke to him, and **he started off.**" John 4:50 "And He said to him, '**Rise**, and go your way; your faith has made you well.'" Luke 17:19*

Let's turn our thoughts back to that OLD TESTAMENT widow. Elijah asked the widow a simple question: "What do you have?" Oil, was the answer. God starts with what we have and adds what we could never come up with. The key instruction given to the widow concerning the jars was, "Do not get a few." And the widow by faith started collecting bottles. Remember there is no miracle yet. There is only raw belief that God is good for His Word. The blessing comes **AFTER the ACTION**. The action is like the baby of faith, it's the part people can see after you've been believing for awhile. It's the visible reflection of your heart. Faith birthed into action is faith indeed.

Remember the story about the man who crossed Niagara Falls with a wheelbarrow on a tight rope? After his first crossing, he asked for volunteers to get into the wheelbarrow. He was going to make a second crossing. Many observers thought that he made sense, *until they had to risk their lives as proof.* You don't really believe God until you're ready to get into the wheelbarrow. James tells us in James 2:17-18 *"Even so faith, **if it has no works, is dead**, being by itself. But someone may well say, 'You have faith, and I have works'; show me your faith without the works, and **I will show you my faith by my works**."*

So you're at the crossroads, staring an apparent contradiction in the face. What do you do? Act on what you believe is truth based on God's Word. Birth the baby of belief and show it to the world. Every time the widow went for more bottles it was at the risk of ridicule. "Why do you need them?" She probably had to explain her situation again and again. It is like Abraham explaining God's promise that he will have descendants without number while folks are looking at his barren, geriatric wife.

It is not at the moment of belief that the answer comes. God knows that belief needs time, like a baby, to be incubated, to grow. Sometimes the best environment for faith to grow is through adversity. It is possible that some of the best "faith" growing time is in the worst of times. Romans 4:20 "Yet, with respect to the promise of God, he did not waver in unbelief, but grew strong in faith, giving glory to God." For big tests, big faith must be nurtured and grown.

Another way the widow's faith is demonstrated is by the number of jars she collects. She is told, "Do not get a few." If she is skeptical, she will save herself a lot of work and embarrassment and just collect what she thinks she can "get by with." But we see that she BELIEVES because she gathers **all that can be found**.

Faith is what opens up the full potential that God offers. God has said to the widow: "How many bottles can you believe me for?" She has responded with a God-sized challenge: all that can be found. Her son says, "**There is not one more.**" Faith is what believes God for all that can be accomplished.

"We fail many times to receive the blessing He has ready for us, because we do not go forward with Him. While we miss much good through not waiting for God, we also miss much through over-waiting. There are times when our strength is to sit still, but there are also times when we are to go forward with a firm step." J.R. Miller, <u>Streams in the Desert</u>, p.37.

Faith results not in sufficiency, but in ABUNDANCE

Faith brings blessings that hard work cannot. Work is what I can do. Faith is found in what only He can do. She had asked "God, can you meet my need?" and hundreds of jars later His response was, "Yes. I am more than enough for your need. I am sufficient for ANY need. I am the abundance that is represented by 12 baskets of leftovers AFTER the multitude is fed (Mark 6:43), 153 fish caught after you caught NOTHING (John 21:11). I am abundance and a vital relationship with me produces blessing. Faith produces blessing. There was enough to pay the bill AND enough left over to live on. There was abundance.

I am not talking here about dollar bills, though that is the form HER abundance took. I am saying that when faith meets a problem, and faith wins, we bring home the spoils of war. There is always an abundance when God-sized abilities meet human sized needs.

Over and over Jesus demonstrated that it's our lack of faith that keeps us lying on a stretcher when we could be walking around (Matthew 9:2), or struggling in the fitful storm when we could be enjoying a calm sea (Matthew 14:26), or stumbling around blindly when we could have our vision restored (Matthew 9:29). Faith brings abundance that we couldn't enjoy any other way. Put a limit on your faith and you automatically put limits on your life. Are you at the Crossroads of Contradiction? Are you asking? Are you acting on your belief? Are you experiencing the abundance of God's response?

9

Waiting on God

Are you in God's waiting room?

You have been praying about something for a long time and see no answer. You are wondering whether you should even keep on asking for this thing. It seems so hopeless. Mrs. Charles Cowman has wisely said *"The problem of getting great things from God is being able to hold on for the last half hour." (<u>Streams in the Desert,</u> p. 81.)*

"Until the time that His word came to pass, the word of the Lord tested him." Psalm 105:19

You never know where you are on God's time line. The answer may come in two minutes or two decades. You don't get a number that gives you the idea of who's next and how long the wait will be. It's not like the post office where you can size up the situation in the waiting room and decide if it's worth it or not. And so in God's waiting room, like the post office, many "prayers" have been discarded simply because those who claimed a promise were not willing to "wait" for their fulfillment.

My friend Terry experienced God's waiting room last year. He and his wife came for prayer on December 16th. Terry was feeling a call to leave his current position but did not have another job offer. After prayers were offered and some applications were sent out, they began to look with anticipation to what the Lord would do for them. No job offers came in during a long period of waiting. By June, Terry was sure God was calling him to a different position, and resigned, but had no assurance of a new job. He now had a daughter on her way to college and funds would be needed to take care of expenses. On July fourth I saw Terry and he told me that God had not only provided a huge gift to help with his daughter's schooling, but also a new position (shortly after his going away party) with less hours and more money. Praise the Lord!

David often found himself in God's waiting room

David was anointed king by the prophet Samuel and then waited years to see it actually come to pass. While in a state of constant movement as he fled for his life he waited for what God had promised. After being anointed king over the tribe of Judah, he waited seven more years to become king over all Israel. He learned to wait in family matters and in matters of state. He waited in grief and he waited in worship. He is a good tour guide for us in the process. (Not that his waiting was **always** in expectant faith. Check out I Sam. 27:1 *"But David thought to himself, 'one of these days I will be destroyed by the hand of Saul. The best thing I can do is to escape to the land of the Philistines.'"* That actually turned out to be one of the worst things he could do. (It is nice to know that even God's heroes had their battles with doubt.)

"And my soul is greatly dismayed; but Thou, O Lord—how long? Return, O Lord, rescue my soul; save me because of Thy lovingkindness. For there is no mention of Thee in death; in Sheol who will give Thee thanks? I am weary with my sighing; every night I make my bed swim, I dissolve my couch with my tears. My eye has wasted away with grief; it has become old because of all my adversaries." Psalm 6:3-7 "Why dost Thou stand afar off, O Lord? Why dost Thou hide Thyself in times of trouble?" Psalm 10:1 "How long, O Lord? Wilt Thou forget me forever? How long wilt Thou hide Thy face from me? How long shall I take counsel in my soul, having sorrow in my heart all the day? How long will my enemy be exalted over me? Consider and answer me, O Lord, my God; enlighten my eyes, lest I sleep the sleep of death." Psalm 13:1-3 "My God, my God, why hast Thou forsaken me? Far from my deliverance are the words of my groaning. O my God, I cry by day, but Thou dost not answer; and by night, but I have no rest." Psalm 22:1-2 "I am weary with my crying; my throat is parched; my eyes fail while I wait for my God." Psalm 69:3

WHAT you wait for is important

The best things in life are worth waiting for. In fact, the following things ONLY come through waiting. Like awaiting the birth of a child, they cannot be grabbed up when WE ARE READY. We must wait until HE IS READY.

"*For Thy salvation I wait*, O Lord." Genesis 49:18 - You can't tell Him when to show up, because it's His salvation! "And thus, having patiently waited, **he obtained the promise**." Hebrews 6:15 - You can't tell Him when to do it, because it's His promise. "For evildoers will be cut off, but those who wait for the Lord, **they will inherit the land**." Psalm 37:9 "The Lord is good to those who wait for Him, to *the person who seeks Him." Lamentations 3:25 "For from of old they have not heard nor perceived by ear, neither has the eye seen a God besides Thee, who acts in behalf of the one who waits for Him." Isaiah 64:4 "The Lord favors those who fear Him, Those who wait for His lovingkindness." Psalm 147:11*

Whom you wait for is important

Can the person you are waiting for be relied on to show up? Do they have a track record you can trust? When I tell my kids they have a doctor's appointment and that I'll be picking them up from school early, they sometimes end up going to the office and asking to use the phone. I have forgotten them on more than one occasion. So there is a sense of distrust. But God ALWAYS shows up ON TIME.

When men from our church were preparing to go back to the orphanage in Uganda, we prepared eighteen plastic tubs of items that we thought would be useful. We had obtained a list of what was needed from Vicki, one of the missionaries. There was one item on the list that she said they could use more than all the others: a push lawn mower. When I mentioned it to my husband and Cal, the team leader, they gave me a lot of good reasons why they wouldn't be able to take it on this trip. It would be too big and bulky. It might cause problems going through customs. All the money for equipment had already been allocated. Where could you even find such a thing these days? All the mowers we saw were gas-powered. It just wasn't going to happen.

The hard thing about faith is that sometimes it can just be stubbornness dressed up to look good. I kept praying about the mower, and the thought that Vicki really felt it was needed made me keep coming back to the Lord. I did a little research on the Internet and found that you could purchase such a mower through Sears for about one hundred twenty dollars. I pressed my husband a little bit about the situation. He was not encouraging. I am trying to be a more submissive wife and I am aware that "promptings" need be tested. So I shared with my friend Marti that I wasn't going to try anymore to convince the guys. But in prayer I kept asking... "Lord, it's just a little mower. It's not too hard for You." You can change their minds. You can provide the funds. You can make a way." It was getting close to the time when the team would leave.

Four days before the team was scheduled to leave, I received a phone call. The caller asked, "Is there anything left that the missionaries need?" "Well, there is one thing they still need, but the guys can't take it." I explained about the mower. They asked, "Could it be mailed?" I had mailed packages to Uganda before and the postage was staggering. I replied, "It's possible, but very expensive." The person responded by saying that they had such and such an amount set aside to do some of God's work. It was right in the ballpark of what I thought it might cost to purchase and mail the mower. I called my husband and asked him if it would be all right to have someone pay for and mail the mower? He was all for it, so I picked up the mower (it came in a nice snug box), took it to the post office and sent it along with some prayer to its destination. The post office had said it would probably take two weeks to arrive. That was good. The team would be there when it came and could see how useful it was to the orphanage.

When the team returned from Uganda one of the first things I asked about was the mower. "It never came," was my hubby's response. Weeks and months went by. Every time I asked the Dangers about it, through E-mail, they had nothing to report, however Vicki mentioned that some times things arrive much later than expected. When you are waiting in prayer for something the only right time to give up is when God says, "No," or the need no longer exists. In

January of 2003, I noticed the entry in my prayer journal about the mower. I was preparing a study on spiritual warfare at the time, so my prayer went something like this: "God, this is YOUR mower. YOU moved me to ask for it. YOU moved the person to donate the money. YOU made a way to get it there and right now THE ENEMY has YOUR mower stuck somewhere where YOUR people cannot benefit from it." I didn't understand why the Lord had pressed me to beseech Him if the mower was never meant to arrive. I have to admit, this prayer was a last ditch effort of faith. A mustard seed would be a good way to describe the size of what I could believe for at that moment.

As I was working on this book the most incredible thing happened. After seven months I received an E-mail from Vicki Dangers. I'm sure you can guess what had happened. The mower had arrived. Nothing was broken and it was immediately put to work. Praise the Lord who has authority over mail, mowers and missionaries!

"And now, Lord, for what do I wait? My hope is in Thee." Psalm 39:7 "And it will be said in that day, 'Behold, this is our God for whom we have waited that He might save us. This is the Lord for whom we have waited; let us rejoice and be glad in His salvation.'" Isaiah 25:9 "I wait for the Lord, my soul does wait, and in His word do I hope." Psalm 130:5

"Above everything, when you wait on God, do so in the spirit of abounding hopefulness. It is God in His glory, in His power, in His love longing to bless you that are waiting." Andrew Murray, <u>Waiting on God</u>, p. 46

We will not be sorry or ashamed

When you take a number at the Post Office and choose to wait in line you can be confident of this: eventually you will receive the help you need. It doesn't matter how long you have to stand in line. Eventually your waiting will be completed and you will hear a voice say "May I help you?" The Post Office isn't some fly-by-night operation. They have a reputation to uphold. So does the Lord God! The omniscient and omnipotent One, opens his window and tells us that all who are willing to wait will find help.

"He invites them to wait on Him and assumes that disappointment is impossible." Andrew Murray, <u>Waiting on God</u>, *p. 110*

Meditate on these verses and pray for something you've been waiting to see fulfilled: *"Indeed, none of those who wait for Thee will be ashamed."* Psalm 25:3a *"Guard my soul and deliver me; do not let me be ashamed, for I take refuge in Thee."* Psalm 25:20 *"In Thee, O Lord, I have taken refuge; let me never be ashamed; in Thy righteousness deliver me."* Psalm 31:1 *"They looked to Him and were radiant, and their faces shall never be ashamed."* Psalm 34:5 *"In Thee, O Lord, I have taken refuge; let me never be ashamed."* Psalm 71:1

HOW you wait is important

There are many times when HOW my girls act while waiting determines HOW LONG they will have to wait. I might mention that we will be going to the store later or suggest a fun activity that we might do as a family. When they wait patiently, trusting me to keep my word, the plan goes forward as planned. But whining and asking are two different modes of communication. I personally despise whining. I think God does too. Whining implies that you have been forgotten and that something due you is being withheld unfairly. God, like a wise parent, usually waits until we realize WHOM we are talking to and HOW we should be addressing Him. He loves it when we wait expectantly with an eye on the door for the things He has promised. But make no mistake, He cannot be goaded into performing on our timetable. His ways are perfect. His reputation is untarnished. Here are ways to wait that get God's attention:

Expectantly – *"But as for me, I will watch expectantly for the Lord; I will wait for the God of my salvation. My God will hear me." Micah 7:7 "And be like men who are waiting for their master when he returns from the wedding feast, so that they may immediately open the door to him when he comes and knocks." Luke 12:36*

"We must depend upon the performance of the promise, when all the ways leading up to it are shut up. For all the promises of God in him are yea (yes) and in him Amen (so be it) unto the glory of God by us!" (II Corinthians 1:20) Matthew Henry

Eagerly – *"Give ear to my words. In the morning I will order my prayer to Thee and eagerly watch." Psalm 5:1a, 3 "But if we hope for what we do not see, with perseverance we wait eagerly for it." Romans 8:25 "Indeed, while following the way of Thy judgments, O Lord, we have waited for Thee eagerly." Isaiah 26:8a "And I will wait for the Lord who is hiding His face from the house of Jacob; I will even look eagerly for Him." Isaiah 8:17 "My soul waits for the Lord more than the watchmen for the morning; indeed, more than the watchmen for the morning." Psalm 130:6*

Confidently – *"I will say to God my rock, 'Why hast Thou forgotten me? Why do I go mourning because of the oppression of the enemy? As a shattering of my bones, my adversaries revile me, while they say to me all day long,*

"Where is your God?' " Why are you in despair, O my soul? And why have you become disturbed within me? Hope in God, for I shall yet praise Him, The help of my countenance, and my God." Psalm 42:9-11 "I will give Thee thanks forever, because Thou hast done it, and I will wait on Thy name, for it is good, in the presence of Thy godly ones." Psalm 52:9

With faithful action - *"Be patient, therefore, brethren, until the coming of the Lord. Behold, the farmer waits for the precious produce of the soil, being patient about it, until it gets the early and late rains." James 5:7 (The farmer doesn't sit by the pool and wait for the harvest. He is faithfully in the field, and while he works, he waits.)*

Continually - *"Therefore, return to your God, observe kindness and justice, and wait for your God continually." Hosea 12:6 (If you get out of line at the post office, you have ceased to "wait.")*

With praise that proceeds the answer – *"Lord, how long wilt Thou look on? Rescue my soul from their ravages, my only life from the lions. I will give Thee thanks in the great congregation; I will praise Thee among a mighty throng." Psalm 35:17-18 (He doesn't have the answer yet, but he's praising as if it had already come.)*

In stillness (resignation of human interference) – *"My soul waits in silence for God only; from Him is my salvation." Psalm 62:1 "Do not say, 'I will repay evil'; wait for the Lord, and He will save you." Proverbs 20:22*

"In being 'still' before God we saturate ourselves in the true condition of ourselves, (spiritually poor) and that of God (infinitely able). While rushing about we still lay claim

in ignorance to the idea that there is something we can do to change the situation on our own. The position of inactivity and the posture of hope puts us in the place of receiving that which only God can do.

"I once thought that after I prayed it was my duty to do everything that I could do to bring the answer to pass. He taught me a better way. He showed me that my self-effort always hindered His working, and that when I prayed and definitely believed Him for anything, He wanted me to wait in the spirit of praise, and only do what He bade me. It seems so unsafe to just sit still, and do nothing but trust the Lord, and the temptation to take the battle into our own hands is often tremendous." Andrew Murray, <u>Waiting on God</u>, *p. 129.*

"We all know how impossible it is to rescue a drowning man who tries to help his rescuer, and it is equally impossible for the Lord to fight our battles for us when we insist upon trying to fight them ourselves. It is not that He will not, but He cannot. Our interference hinders His working." C.H.P., <u>Streams in the Desert</u>, *p. 131.*

"Spiritual forces cannot work while earthly forces are active." J.H.M., <u>Streams in the Desert</u>, *p. 131.*

"'Stand still'—keep the posture of an upright man, ready for action, expecting further orders, cheerfully and patiently awaiting the directing voice; and it will not be long ere God shall say to you as distinctly as Moses said it to the people of Israel, 'Go forward.'" Charles Spurgeon, <u>Streams in the Desert</u>, *p. 132.*

Abraham's wife, Sarah, would have done well had she learned this lesson. She felt that she needed to help God fulfill His "long awaited" promise to her husband. If she had understood this spiritual lesson there would not be two nations at the center of world conflict right now. Think about the destructive consequences that might affect your world, and the far-reaching effects of them if you do not learn to wait on the Lord.

At the center of this weakness is a wrong concept of who we are and who God is. If He is weak, and we are strong, then we must assist Him in His work. But as we come to know the truth more clearly, we see it is through Him, the Mighty One, that the strength, the action, and the timing of fulfillment comes.

"There is nothing so masterly as inactivity in some things, and there is nothing so hurtful as restless working, for God has undertaken to work His sovereign will." A. B. Simpson, <u>Streams in the Desert</u>, p. 215.

So waiting furthers our relationship with and dependence on God and the work of His Holy Spirit. We must get a daily dose of courage and trust to go further. If you are trying to humanly bolster your own faith you will fail. But let the Word of God, which reflects His will for your life, pour over your request and either your request will change, along with your heart, or you will have the thing you have asked for.

We must wait in order to hear
God speak (for marching orders)

If we could see how much trouble we cause by moving ahead when God is still trying to teach us to be still, we would be ashamed. Think of the implications for boards and committees who think God's job is to perform by THEIR deadlines. How different the decision-makers of the New Testament went about their work. We see the early church leaders ministering to the Lord through prayer and fasting and HE responds by tapping them on the head with a missionary plan. The more we come to know who God is, the more we will be able to rest in the process.

I enjoy the encounter between Jesus and His mother at the wedding of Cana. Mary does not try to use human methods to get more wine. She doesn't send James and Jude to the market. She just says to the servant with quiet trust, "Do whatever He tells you." If we could learn this one truth: to do what He tells us, not more, not less, then our churches would save time, energy and money that is wasted by our fretful impatience. But to hear, we must wait. And to wait we must believe.

Meditate on these verses in your prayer time today: *"Moses therefore said to them, 'Wait, and I will listen to what the Lord will command concerning you.' Then the Lord spoke to Moses, saying..." Numbers 9:8-9 "And you shall go down before me to Gilgal; and behold, I will come down to you to offer burnt offerings and sacrifice peace offerings. You shall wait seven days until I come to you and show you what you should do." I Samuel 10:8 "Lead me in Thy truth and teach me, for Thou art the God of my salvation; for Thee I wait all the day." Psalm 25:5 "Blessed is the man who listens to me, watching daily at my gates, waiting at my doorposts." Proverbs 8:34 "My soul languishes for Thy salvation; I wait for Thy word." Psalm 119:81 "I rise before dawn and cry for help; I wait for Thy words." Psalm 119:147 "They quickly forgot His works; they did not wait for His counsel." Psalm 106:13*

"And so, while we think that we know and trust the power of God for what we may expect we may be hindering Him by not giving time and not definitely cultivating the habit of waiting for His counsel." Andrew Murray, <u>Waiting on God</u>*, p. 80.*

The darkroom of waiting produces God's best work

God does His best work in the dark. Like a photographer in a darkroom, he prefers the blackness that hides His deeds until the development of "answer" and "recipient" is complete. When you find yourself sitting in the dark, remember that God is working. You may not see the work. But to see it too soon would destroy its ultimate beauty. Some things cannot be completed without the elements of darkness and hiddenness.

"Waiting, even in darkness, is unconscious advance, because it is God you have to do with, and He is working in you." Andrew Murray, <u>Waiting on God</u>, p. 147.

"Don't steal tomorrow out of God's hands. Give God time to speak to you and reveal His will. He is never too late, learn to wait." Mrs. Charles Cowman, <u>Streams in the Desert</u>, p. 101.

"When God delays, He is not inactive. He is getting ready His instruments, He is ripening our powers; and at the appointed moment we shall arise equal to our task." Dr. Jowett, <u>Streams in the Desert</u>, p. 100.

There was a period of time, while serving on one church staff, that I longed to be at a different church. I loved a church and school in Escondido, California, but God was doing a great work in Garden Grove, California and I ached to be a part of this great work (This church was experiencing the results of deeper prayer.) It was a secret prayer of mine, stuffed way down inside my heart, and never voiced out loud until one day, at a pastor's meeting. The pastor of this very church started hinting around that he would like to have me on his staff. There weren't too many children's pastors in our denomination at the time, and they needed someone to take on the challenge of working with hundreds of children. He talked as if I might hear from him any day with an offer. Immediately, this heart's desire went on my prayer list. That meeting had been held in the early fall. Month after month I prayed and beseeched God for the opportunity to go to this exciting venue of ministry. Month after month I heard nothing from the pastor. In the spring I began to be concerned. My teaching contract would be up and I would be asked if I was going to return for the following year. If I were to leave I would have to sell my mobile home. This would not be easy. This was one of the first things I had to believe God for without seeing any action for a long period of time. During these weeks and months my faith deepened. I had a sense that I would be leaving, but there was nothing to actually see. I gave notice that I would not be returning. I believe that was in March. This was a scary thing to do, but it was an act of faith. Finally the call came in June. The pastor asked, "How quickly can you be here?" By the month of July, I was in my new ministry position, God took care of selling my mobile home and I had acquired a deeper faith in LONG-TERM prayer.

The development of character through endurance

The very process of continuing in hardship and waiting produces what no other thing can: a pearl, a pearl of perfected character. In this developmental process, the grain of irritation is like not getting what we want or think we need. The secretion that is poured out by the stance of continuous waiting on God soothes the irritation of the flesh and coats it. It makes the trial bearable and produces a jewel in our character that cannot come from any other source. The final rescue or answer pales in comparison to what has been worked into us on the journey.

"The word 'patience' is derived from the Latin word for suffering." Andrew Murray, <u>Waiting on God</u>, p. 72.

"Knowing that the testing of your faith produces endurance. And let endurance have its perfect result, that you may be perfect and complete, lacking in nothing." James 1:3-4 "For you have need of endurance, so that when you have done the will of God, you may receive what was promised." Hebrews 10:36 "Behold, we count those blessed who endured. You have heard of the endurance of Job and have seen the outcome of the Lord's dealings, that the Lord is full of compassion and is merciful." James 5:11

The sin of impatience hinders God's work

When our first daughter was due to be born after nine months of waiting, I was ready. Day after day she failed to keep her appointment for delivery. I suffered more than most with Braxton-Hicks' (false labor pain) and never having experienced the difference between these pains and real labor, we ended up going to the hospital six times before her actual birth. The nurses were kind, and even though my pains were powerful, after drinking some juice and resting, they would subside and I was sent home empty-handed. I remember thinking on one trip, "I'm not leaving this time without a baby." But no matter how much I wanted to hold her in my arms God wasn't finished with her yet. She finally arrived two weeks overdue and practically had to be pried out. (When we talk about all the trips to the hospital my strong-willed child jokes that she was comfy and wasn't ready to be born yet.)

God meets us in the labor room of prayer every time we arrive. But it's only when He's good and ready to reveal His perfect handiwork that we leave with the answer. Be patient, His answers are masterpieces of intricate handiwork. You won't be disappointed.

"Fret not thyself. Do not get unduly heated! Keep cool! Even in a good cause, fretfulness is not a wise helpmeet. Fretting only heats the bearings; it does not generate the steam. It is no help to a train for the axles to get hot. Their heat is only a hindrance. When the axles get heated, it is because of unnecessary friction; dry surfaces are grinding together, which ought to be kept in smooth cooperation by a delicate cushion of oil." Mrs. Charles Cowman, The Silver Lining

Each moment of waiting
puts us one step closer to the answer

"Prayer which takes the fact that past prayers have not been answered as a reason for languor, has already ceased to be the prayer of faith. To the prayer of faith the fact that prayers remain unanswered is only evidence that the moment of the answer is so much nearer." William Arthur

Every prayer we utter brings us one step closer to the prize we wait for. No matter how many paces there are on the route to the treasure, each one brings us closer than the one before. As we wait for revival in our city we KNOW that it will come. Each Saturday evening of obedience brings us one prayer closer. Each month of faithfulness scoots us along in our journey. Every year of pleading propels us onward toward the victory.

Waiting wrings the self out of us
so that we may be filled with more of Him

"True patience is the losing of our self-will in His perfect will." Andrew Murray, Waiting on God, p. 73.

During a time of great hurt I would come to the Lord morning after morning looking for His relief and comfort. It would be years before I could make any sense out of the situation and see its good. But every morning as I waited for a change in my circumstances, the Lord did some changing in me. He pointed out the truth in some criticism I had received. He showed me places in my heart that no one else could even see that needed cleansing and healing. He was getting at something far more important than my comfort. He was working on holiness.

Our lives, while waiting, are an encouragement to others

"May those who fear Thee see me and be glad, because I wait for Thy word." Psalm 119:74 "May those who wait for Thee not be ashamed through me, O Lord God of hosts; may those who seek Thee not be dishonored through me, O God of Israel." Psalm 69:6

One of the shows I enjoy most is Candid Camera. I love it when they do a feature on people waiting to be helped. They might have the lights turning off automatically in the waiting room (to save energy) or the customer taking a number in the hundreds (while others are getting numbers in single digits). It's fun to watch people get impatient. Surprisingly, however, sometimes we see someone who has incredible patience. They are kept waiting for a long time in a restaurant or they watch others (who haven't waited as long as they have) go into the doctor before them. Some people display incredible kindness to the workers. We watch in wonder at their capacity to wait and it touches us. Suddenly, instead of laughing at them, we feel compelled to hang a medal around their neck.

When you are waiting for God's answers to your prayers you are being watched by many that have tuned in to see how your life will turn out. There is no sermon that will be heard as clearly as the one you preach with your patience. No billboard is as eye-catching as when you are in trouble. No jingle will be as memorable as the tune your life whistles out while you wait.

A friend of mine, now a well-known Christian author, spent many years as a single mom on a limited income. Her taxman saw her faithfulness to tithing long before she ever sold a book and began to receive its royalties. He told her much later, after her situation had changed for the better, "Do you know when your faith had the greatest impact on my life? It wasn't after things got easy for you and your son. It was watching you trust the Lord when you had nothing." Wait with patience and you will have the chance to impact hundreds who are waiting to see what will happen in the next episode of your life.

"His eye is on those who wait. Such are God's waiting ones. And now, think of the God on whom we wait. 'The eye of the Lord is on them that fear him, on them that hope in His mercy; to deliver their soul from death, and to keep them alive in famine.' Not to prevent the danger of death and famine-this is often needed to stir up to wait on Him-but to deliver and keep alive. For the dangers are often very real and dark; the situation, whether in the temporal or spiritual life, may appear to be utterly hopeless. There is always one hope; God's eye is on them." Andrew Murray, <u>Waiting on God</u>, p. 57.

The end result of waiting is receiving

Who cares how long you had to wait when you finally get what you were waiting for? I remember trying to reupholster an old couch we had in our front room. It cost one hundred dollars just to buy the fabric and within a few minutes of finishing it I was not happy with the results. I had walked through furniture stores and seen what new couches cost and knew that even if we had the money it would not be allocated for something to sit on. That day I began praying that the Lord would give us some better furniture for our living room. I even described them to the Lord, just in case He had trouble figuring out exactly what I thought would look best. At that time I had already painted my living room walls gold (anticipating the reupholstered furniture that was brown). I prayed regularly for more than a year over that simple prayer request. One day a friend from church called and asked if we would like their living room furniture? I said "Yes" before I even asked what color it was. The set was lovely, but was sort of a blue gray shade. I was grateful to my friend and to the Lord and I took it with eagerness. But all the time I was wishing the set could go in our family room, (blue and burgundy), and that we could get a different set for the living room, to go with the brown and gold. Another year or so went by. (I actually have the dates marked on my prayer list to note the length of time this took.) One day I got a call. "Are you going to be home Friday?" a friend asked. "Why?" I inquired. "Something's going to be delivered." I kid you not! That Friday when the moving van arrived in front of my house, I didn't even know WHAT they were delivering. But it didn't take long to find out. There was a beautiful living room set in browns and golds. It was a gift from the Lord, but through a friend with His heart. The bluish gray set was moved to the family room where it gave us much pleasure and I got to get rid of the old horrid couch I hated. Just ask me if it was worth it to pray for over 2 years to get new furniture. Of course it was. When I realized how good God had been to meet a simple, fleshly desire like furniture, I began to think, "I need to pray about stuff that REALLY matters, because

God is ready to answer my prayers." If He can deliver brown and gold sofas, then He can bring salvation and revival with no effort.

"I was crying to the Lord with my voice, and He answered me from His holy mountain." Psalm 3:4 "I waited patiently for the Lord; and He inclined to me, and heard my cry." Psalm 40:1

10

Warring Through Prayer

"And He caused His people to be very fruitful, and made them stronger than their adversaries." Psalm 105:24

Go to war for your family

Right now our country stands poised and ready to go to war. There are daily debates about whether now is the right time or whether more "diplomatic talk" is necessary. Most people can agree on at least one thing: there are some things **worth** going to war over. Your family is one of them. There is never a convenient time for war, but when we see the lives of our family being pillaged by the enemy, we too must pick up our sword and fight. As we walk through some truths about spiritual warfare, I ask you to contemplate the words of Nehemiah as he encouraged the wall builders: *"Remember the Lord who is great and awesome, **and fight** for your brothers, your sons, your daughters, your wives, and your houses." Nehemiah 4:14b*

Satan loves to attack the households of God's people. This is where he sometimes finds us vulnerable. His methods vary. He may try using sickness. He may employ disharmony. This is why we must constantly be putting to good use the twenty-four hour security system of warring prayer.

"But be sure of this, that if the head of the house had known at what time of the night the thief was coming, he would have been on the alert and would not have allowed his house to be broken into." Matthew 24:43

Jesus uses this parable to show us that we can either leave the doors and windows wide open (through prayerlessness) and be surprised by the inevitable, a thief (Satan) breaking in, or we can be in a constant state of alertness *at the window,* and secure it's vulnerability. Each night my husband physically checks all the doors and windows of our house and prays safety over us all. It's a wonderful habit. You too can come to the Lord Jesus each day, put on your spiritual armor, and lock out the enemy's pilfering of the treasures of God in your care, your children.

You are the gatekeeper over God's treasures

I was fascinated by a study of the gatekeepers' role in the Old Testament. One third of all priests had an unusual duty. They were the security guards over God's treasures. It's true! Their office is described as an office of trust and they were to open the doors every morning and close them every night. There were valuable items in God's house and He wanted them protected, so one in three priests stood guard duty.

"'This is the thing which you shall do: one third of you, of the priests and Levites who come in on the Sabbath, shall

*be gatekeepers, and one third shall be at the king's house, and a third at the Gate of the Foundation; and all the people shall be in the courts of the house of the Lord.' And he stationed all the people, each man with his weapon in his hand, from the right side of the house to the left side of the house, by the altar and by the house, around the king." II Chronicles 23:4, 10 "For the four chief gatekeepers who were Levites, were in **an office of trust**, and were over the chambers and **over the treasuries in the house of God.** And they spent the night around the house of God, **because the watch was committed to them**; and they were **in charge of opening it morning by morning**." I Chronicles 9:26-2 "And I searched for a man among them who should build up the wall and stand in the gap before Me for the land, **that I should not destroy it**; but I found no one." Ezekiel 22:30 "And there is no one who calls on Thy name, **who arouses himself to take hold of Thee**." Isaiah 64:7a "It has been made a desolation, desolate, it mourns before Me; the whole land has been made desolate, because no man lays it to heart**." Jeremiah 12:11*

Can you imagine what it might have felt like to have been a security guard on duty September 11th? What if it had been your duty that day to search the passengers at one of the airports where those infamous flights took off? Can you imagine going to bed at night with the thought that your carelessness might have allowed such a tragedy?

God has given each of us an office of trust. He has placed us within families, churches and nations for a reason. He wants us to intercede daily for protection and to solicit spiritual resources for those we are responsible for: the treasures with which we have been charged.

Shortly after 9/11 another terrorist tried to board a plane with explosives in his shoes. Do you remember hearing about this on the news? However, he was quickly apprehended. The attitude of the security guards had changed dramatically in just a few hours. Somebody was in a state of alertness, and that readiness paid off.

Meditate on these verses that encourage alertness in your prayer life: *"Take heed, **keep on the alert**; for you do not know when the appointed time is. It is like a man, away on a journey, who upon leaving his house and putting his slaves in charge, assigning to each one his task, also commanded the doorkeeper **to stay on the alert. Therefore, be on the alert**— for you do not know when the master of the house is coming, whether in the evening, at midnight, at cockcrowing, or in the morning— lest he come suddenly and **find you asleep**. And what I say to you I say to all, '**Be on the alert!**'" Mark 13:33-37 "**But keep on the alert at all times**, praying in order that you may have strength to escape all these things that are about to take place, and to stand before the Son of Man." Luke 21:36 "**Therefore be on the alert**, remembering that night and day for a period of three years **I did not cease to admonish each one with tears**." Acts 20:31 "Devote yourselves to prayer, **keeping alert in it** with an attitude of thanksgiving." Colossians 4:2 "So then let us not sleep as others do, **but let us be alert and sober**." I Thessalonians 5:6 "Be of sober spirit, **be on the alert**. Your adversary, the devil, prowls about like a roaring lion, seeking someone to devour." I Peter 5:8*

When we pray, things happen

We enjoyed a drama at church that helps me picture what happens when I pray for my children and my husband. In it, a young woman prays protection over her son at the bus stop (it's not a great neighborhood) and for her marriage (she and her husband don't have much time together and funds are limited). In response to each request we see "Murray," an angelic dispatcher, answer God's red phone and dispatch angelic couriers. An angel is sent to watch over her son in the form of a neighbor looking out the window. A grandma-type angel is planted next door who receives instructions to baby-sit once a month so the couple can have more time together. All these are in response to her quiet prayer, but when she gets up from her knees, she cannot see the events that have been put into motion and concludes, "Nothing ever happens when I pray!" To this, "Murray" the angelic dispatcher who has been trying to keep up with all the requests for dispatching, throws up his hands in frustration. When we take the time to fight for our family we may not see the results right away either. But make up your mind to keep "Murray" busy with your requests. The Lord God is listening to every heart's cry and is ready to act on our behalf.

"Then Israel sent messengers to Sihon, king of the Amorites, saying, 'Let me pass through your land. We will not turn off into field or vineyard; we will not drink water from wells. We will go by the king's highway until we have passed through your border.' But Sihon would not permit Israel to pass through his border. So Sihon gathered all his people and went out against Israel in the wilderness, and came to Jahaz and fought against Israel. Then Israel struck him with the edge of the sword, and took possession of his land from the Arnon to the Jabbok, as far as the sons of Ammon; for the border of the sons of Ammon was Jazer. And Israel took all these cities and Israel lived in all the cities of the Amorites, in Heshbon, and in all her villages." Numbers 21:21-25

Sometimes God's ultimate goal in allowing spiritual warfare is not immediate comfort but long-term blessing. (As in the case with Job.) The Lord allows the enemy to contend with us so that we can defeat his work in this area of our lives and possess greater blessings. When the Israelites ask permission to pass through the land of the idolatrous Amorites, their king refuses, and God does not intervene, it is not because the Lord does not love the Israelites. He is looking farther down the road than providing His people with a sight-seeing tour through town. He wants God honoring Israelites living in the houses of those who have bowed to idols of stone and sticks. He wants more people standing at the doorway of the tent of meeting, like Moses. So the king responds with a loud, "NO!," to Moses' polite request to pass through. And so, the next time you feel the enemy is breathing down your neck, forget about politely passing around his strongholds and supply depots. Start thinking and praying like an Israelite and check out his resources. They might be yours by Monday morning.

Fight for what is yours

My friend Kathy is one of God's best servants. She prays faithfully several times each week for revival in our city. She marches around the abortion clinic each month claiming God's promises over the lives of the unborn. In short, she is sold out to God and His purposes in her life. One night, as we prayed for our city in the cold, winter air, she asked us all to pray for her cat, Delilah who hadn't come home during the last twenty-four hour period. There are times when you just feel God's will in a situation. As Kathy shared with us how special this cat was to her, and the comfort it gave her, I began to feel that even this simple situation was a time to "take back" something that belonged to one of God's people. We prayed together, believing God would answer.

The next morning I was again prompted by the Lord to intercede for...a cat. It might seem funny to some that are reading this, but I had seen this woman go through plenty of difficulties because she stood up for her faith. She had stood tall through slander, an unsubstantiated lawsuit and even threats on her life. She just didn't need this too. I called to ask if there had been any progress. "No, Delilah still hasn't come home." There was more prayer offered up.

Two days later I got a call. Delilah had been found, wounded, but alive. She had apparently been in a fight and had crawled into their shed. (Kathy had not thought to look in a locked shed.) We rejoiced in the fact that we worship a God great enough to care for sparrows, and powerful enough to return cats.

*"And when Abram heard that his relative had been taken captive, **he led out his trained men**, born in his house, three hundred and eighteen, **and went in pursuit** as far as Dan. And he divided his forces against them by night, he and his servants, and defeated them, and pursued them as far as Hobah, which is north of Damascus. **And he brought back all the goods, and also brought back his relative Lot with his possessions, and also the women, and the people."** Genesis 14:14-16*

Prayer journal entry:

12/11/01 My friend Leslie wrote to say her son Brian suddenly died after having a routine surgical procedure performed. Brian is a twin and the family was devastated by the sudden loss. I groan in prayer for God's comfort for his family.

11/0/02 Leslie came out to California for a visit. During our time together she related all the wonderful ways God had comforted their family after Brian's death. (It drew his twin brother back to the Lord!)

"Temptation often comes upon a man with its strongest power when he is nearest to God." Mrs. Charles Cowman,

Streams in the Desert, p. 123.

"To be left unmolested by Satan is no evidence of blessing." Mrs. Charles Cowman, *Streams in the Desert*, p. 122.

Recovering the enemy's strongholds

One objective of war is to recover areas where the enemy has become entrenched. We want to take back ground that he has claimed as his own. There are two ways to approach a spiritual stronghold. The first is to take your stand and fight. We see this method being used in I Chronicles 11:14 "And they took their stand in the midst of the plot, and defended it, and struck down the Philistines; and the Lord saved them by a great victory." *Another way to deal with the situation is to give up and run away:* "When all the men of Israel who were in the valley saw that they had fled, and that Saul and his sons were dead, they forsook their cities and fled; and the Philistines came and lived in them." *I Chronicles 10:7*

The Lord wants us to stand and fight when our circumstances are not living up to God's intentions. Ed Silvoso deals with this topic extensively in his book **That None Should Perish**. You may see in Scripture what a godly marriage is supposed to be like, but no matter what you try, yours falls short. You may read godly parenting principles, but they don't seem to be working on your children. You begin to exist in a state of hopelessness. God doesn't like it when his children live like prisoners instead of conquerors. So He plants passages like this one to tell us to go after what the enemy thinks is his.

"Then Jonathan said to the young man who was carrying his armor, 'Come and let us cross over to the garrison of these uncircumcised; perhaps the Lord will work for us, for

*the Lord is not restrained to save by many or by few.' And his armor bearer said to him, '**Do all that is in your heart**; turn yourself, and **here I am with you according to your desire**.'" I Samuel 14:6-7*

God's purpose on this particular day is to annihilate the enemy, not just help Jonathan and his armor bearer to avoid them. As I meditated on this passage I saw two applications to my prayer life. Let's picture me in Jonathon's place with God as **my** armor bearer. God tells me that the things I desire (godly desires) can be pursued with the confidence that He is right behind me with His power. However, if I switch the two identities and realize that God has His own ideas of how situations should be made right, things become more interesting. As God's servant, like the armor bearer, I can offer up *the desire* that implores Him to line up *my requests* with *His plans* for the day. Then all warfare prayers, no matter how outrageous, can be granted. This is because they would line up with God's will and heart.

*"And in the same way the Spirit also helps our weakness; for we do not know how to pray as we should, but the Spirit Himself intercedes for us with groanings too deep for words; and He who searches the hearts knows what the mind of the Spirit is, because **He intercedes for the saints according to the will of God."** Romans 8:26-27*

When our church chose to participate in Dr. Dobson's *Adopt a Leader* prayer program, I selected Senator Ashcroft as the leader I would pray for and I did it faithfully. I even wrote him verses of encouragement in a card each month. When his name was submitted for Attorney General, there was such a controversy! I remembered hearing a radio interview where Senator Diane Feinstein said words to the effect that his confirmation would be, "over my dead body" because of his pro-life stance. As I prayed specifically for him on January 28, 2001 it seemed similar to the situation of David and Goliath. Here was a puny senator telling God that she could keep Him from doing something. I had a strong impression from the Lord that he would be approved and immediately sent off a note to encourage him with that thought. Four days later, on Feb. 1st, we heard that he was approved. I received a nice note much later from him thanking me for my encouragement. That morning, I got to be God's armor bearer and He had in mind to rearrange the enemy's camp.

Revealing the enemy's tactics

One of the greatest advantages to fighting **God's** battles is that you have an omniscient informant who can let you in on the enemy's tactics. *Ephesians 5:11 "And do not participate in the unfruitful deeds of darkness, **but instead even expose them**."* God can show you, through His Word, how the devil will try to test you. We read about this in the following passage.

*"Now the king of Aram was warring against Israel; and he counseled with his servants saying, 'In such and such a place shall be my camp.' And the man of God sent word to the king of Israel saying, '**Beware that you do not pass this place**, for the Arameans are coming down there.' And the king of Israel sent to the place about which the man of God had told him; thus he warned him, **so that he guarded himself there, more than once or twice**. Now the heart of the king of Aram was enraged over this thing; and he called his servants and said to them, 'Will you tell me which of us is for the king of Israel?' And one of his servants said, 'No, my lord, O king; but Elisha, the prophet who is in Israel, tells the king of Israel the words that you speak in your bedroom.' " II Kings 6:8-12*

Satan's Tactic: Create a misleading sense of reality

Over years of ministry I have seen one tactic that Satan uses again and again. He creates a facade, or false sense of reality for Christians in an effort to get them to act in a wrong way (thereby creating new problems). It's like you're watching a movie where the actors are on a country road and then suddenly the backdrop parts and you see that they are really just on a movie set, far from the country. If Satan can create a false set of circumstances for you to believe, and then get you to act on those false circumstances, he can coax you to sin. For example, a young woman told me that several families didn't like her family and that she witnessed them quieting down when she came near. She was absolutely convinced that they were gossiping about her. This is so like our sneaky enemy. He got her to believe this, then begin to act out of hurt by avoiding those families (creating tension in their relationship). Later on, she left the church. This caused tremendous pain in the body of Christ. Everyday Satan is trying to get you and me to believe his lies so that we will miss the good things that God has prepared for us down the highway of life. We must allow God's Word to accurately align our thinking.

"Never, ever determine the truth of a situation by looking at the circumstances." Henry Blackaby, <u>Experiencing God</u>, p. 100

Satan's Tactic: Attack the character of God

Many times Satan attacks **who God is**. (If He's that powerful, why doesn't he end wickedness? If He's that just, why do good people suffer? If He's wise, why doesn't He tell you how to avoid pain?) Since the enemy knows his Bible just well enough to deliver half its truth, we must be well grounded in the Word in order to counteract his plots. You will find an extensive study on the character qualities of God at our website: www.oliveleafpublications.com. This will help you **counter** his assaults.

Satan's Tactic: Attack who you are in Christ

Another method the devil uses is to attack the very idea of **who we are** in Christ. He mutters, "You are worthless, you are unloved, etc." And here is some truth to remind yourself of when he tries to come in this way. *Luke 12:7 "Indeed, the very hairs of your head are all numbered. Do not fear; **you are of more value than many sparrows**." Zechariah 2:8 "For thus says the Lord of hosts, 'After glory He has sent me against the nations which plunder you, **for he who touches you, touches the apple of His eye.'"***

Satan's Tactic: Add or remove resources/possessions

The enemy may also try to mess with our **resources or possessions**. You may experience testing in the adding as well as the removing of things. The key to counteracting this method is seen in how Job approaches it. Job responds by submitting to God's ultimate authority over "adding and removing" to his life. He fought the attack with this truth. *Job 1:21 "And he said, 'Naked I came from my mother's womb, and naked I shall return there. The Lord gave and the Lord has taken away. Blessed be the name of the Lord.'"* We should do the same.

Our family faced an interesting problem a few years ago. My father had graciously given my husband a beautiful blue Lincoln to drive. Then, as a result of the car accident you read about earlier, my mother gave us her luxurious white Lincoln Towncar. We are simple people and immediately this became a prayer request that went on the list. "Lord, do you want us to keep these cars?" was the prayer that I entered under May 31, 2001.

I struggled over this because the white car had been so special to my father. There is a great story that tells why it was such a meaningful blessing to him, and to me. When my dad got saved, he worked at Ford Motor Co. in Detroit. Until then, he had enjoyed two loves: my mom and new cars. Shortly after his conversion, he had felt the Lord calling him into the ministry and he responded to that call with a total willingness. He only asked that the Lord would not let him down in caring for the needs of His family. When my mom shares how she would make three complete meals out of one pound of hamburger during that time, I don't think that the needs of his family were that demanding! But like most of us, the hunger for other things cost him some grief. My dad wanted "just one more new car" before he entered the ministry.

The situation caused him and my mother to go into debt. Since this was years before the availability of credit cards, my dad ended up going to one bank to pay another. Finally he admitted his wrong decision to the Lord, asked family friends to help, and gained some valuable wisdom. I always thought my dad was just wise from the start, but by sharing this difficult situation he showed me that he had earned every bit of wisdom he ever got.

After the agony of paying that debt back and the humiliation of having to ask friends for help, my dad vowed he would never again be enslaved to a car. He kept that promise. Anyone who knew my dad knew he loved cars, but the Lord helped him enjoy that love by buying and driving older cars. He loved to find a bargain and many, MANY times the cars he purchased ended up being gifts for family or friends in ministry.

Now picture the years of faithful ministry and all the times my dad, in obedience, walked away from the car showroom window. Then, let me encourage you by the final chapter in my dad's life. Not long before he died my dad got a beautiful gift from a generous family member, which is another great story all by itself.

My Aunt Alice, who had worked diligently for a doctor all her life (over 50 years) was named in his will (he had no children). She received a quarter of a million dollars! She had not owned her beautiful, white Lincoln Towncar long, but this huge gift warranted a celebration, so she bought a new car and you can tell by now who got the white one...my dad. He loved that car. As a retired pastor, he had served in churches all over America and during this period he pastored a church in Northern California while maintaining his home in Southern California. Nobody could understand why a pastor would do that. But I understood. First, he got to preach (something that gets under your skin when you've been called to it) and second, he got to drive *that car*. The Lord had rewarded him for a life of faithfulness with the desire of his heart. And I, the generation to follow, got to enjoy the blessings of a godly heritage. We are told in four different verses that God sees the right decisions we make for Him and blesses our families for the next 1,000 generations.

"For I, the Lord your God, am a jealous God, visiting the iniquity of the fathers on the children, and on the third and the fourth generations of those who hate Me, but showing lovingkindness to thousands, to those who love Me and keep My commandments." Deuteronomy 5:9-10 "Know therefore that the Lord your God, He is God, the faithful God, who keeps His covenant and His lovingkindness to a thousandth generation with those who love Him and keep His commandments." Deuteronomy 7:9 "He has remembered His covenant forever, The word which He commanded to a thousand generations." Psalm 105:8 "Remember His covenant forever, the word which He commanded to a thousand generations." I Chronicles 16:15

This is one reason I was finding it difficult to sell this car. I couldn't care less what I drive, but the symbolism of this one was so meaningful. The other reason I didn't want to sell it is that I didn't want to portray to the world that following Christ always ends up being a life of sacrifice. To not display the goodness of God is a distorted picture of God. I agree with Mrs. Hudson Taylor, I have never made a sacrifice for the sake of the gospel that did not return greater blessings to me. At the same time, we knew that it might be difficult for people just joining our church to understand how a pastor, who preached sacrificial living to the Lord, could own two Lincolns.

We can't read God's mind and so the journey of submission is always interesting. We prayed regularly over both cars and tried to keep our will and our hands off of God's decision. (There is a principle George Mueller taught on prayer that is "praying around the table." You picture the situation on a table and then pray all the different ways God might decide to answer your need.) Then in January of 2002 the answer came. A woman rammed through an intersection and hit my husband (in the blue car at the time). The insurance check helped us buy a little Toyota and this brought peace about keeping the white car. The key to responding to the adding of resources is to be content with or without them. This disarms the enemy's attempt to distract or delude us in our walk.

"Not that I speak from want; for I have learned to be content in whatever circumstances I am. I know how to get along with humble means, and I also know how to live in prosperity; in any and every circumstance I have learned the secret of being filled and going hungry, both of having abundance and suffering need." Philippians 4:11-12

A few years ago a leader in our congregation approached

my husband with a problem. He was short fifteen hundred dollars on his house payment and needed a short term loan for two weeks. He asked if the church ever helped people out in this way. My husband responded that no, that would be an illegal use of church funds. The gentleman went on to ask if we *personally* could make him the loan. Looking back there are so many things that we should have done differently. We didn't sit down as a couple to pray about the situation. We didn't discuss and pray over the situation with his wife. (We found out later that she didn't even know he had borrowed the money.) And most important of all, we should have realized that we were not in a position to lend fifteen hundred dollars because we didn't have it. Since the man had said that he only needed it for two weeks we wrote him a check off our credit card. Being debt free was a way of life for us, but this began a two-year long lesson. Of course the couple moved away without paying us back. I'm sure you saw that coming. Every month we tried to tackle this huge amount, which socked us with high interest and grew out of control. Still we knew in our hearts that even though we had done so many wrong things in the situation, God could see our hearts and that we had tried in our own limited way to care for our brother and to do what we could. He knew our hearts had attempted to align with His Word.

"If there is a poor man with you, one of your brothers, in any of your towns in your land which the Lord your God is giving you, you shall not harden your heart, nor close your hand from your poor brother; but you shall freely open your hand to him, and shall generously lend him sufficient for his need in whatever he lacks." Deuteronomy 15:7-8

Day after day I would meet God at the window. I was armed with a ton of verses about victory over financial problems. My favorite one in this particular trial was the verse that tells us we can say to this mountain: "Be removed!" I can guarantee you that everyday I asked the Lord to get rid of this financial nightmare. I knew that the enemy wanted to keep us bound and discouraged. I knew God wanted us to learn from our mistakes and not be enslaved to the enemy's tricks. So I prayed. One day, a family member offered to give an amount that cleared up the entire situation. This story has encouraged others that, under a heavy load, financial or otherwise, has needed to know that God can move their mountain too.

Prayer journal entry:

3/2000 The loan was made.
7/19/01 Prayed over debt. (Scriptural truth put into action: "I see nothing." "Go back.")
9/17/01 The debt is completely taken care of.

Prayer journal entry:

11/2 We have had some unexpected expenses and have about eight hundred dollars in bills.
10/11 A bookkeeping error resulted in us getting an additional nine hundred dollars in salary. (This was money that had been earned, but when a new bookkeeping system had been installed an error had been made and we were owed back pay.) What a coincidence!

Satan's Attack: Touching our health

The enemy may touch our **health** (as seen in Job's encounter). God must allow it and that means that He knows He can bring us victoriously through it. But some health problems are not meant to stick around. They are simply allowed to be object lessons in God's ability to remove them. *"But when Jesus heard it, He said, 'This sickness is not unto death, but for the glory of God, that the Son of God may be glorified by it.'" John 11:4*

Do you remember the woman who was sick for eighteen years? She might have come to women's Bible study every week with the same prayer request and yet remained sick. But Jesus put His finger right on the trouble. The root of this particular illness was a demon. I am learning in my prayer life not to accept sickness routinely. My role is to ask God to heal it. My duty is to treat it with spiritual tools as well as physical ones. My responsibility is not to give up in the asking. God's responsibility is to decide what is best.

Several years ago, my husband went on a mission trip to the Philippines and returned with a parasite in his stomach. This caused an acid-reflux condition to develop and the result is that my husband can no longer enjoy fruit (his favorite food). We have been praying for the Lord to heal this for many years, and I am not giving up. I want to complete my part of the prayer process. If God never heals him, then I will know that it is because my gracious shepherd knows better what will give Him glory. But one day the New Testament woman, who was mentioned earlier and had been sick, showed up at Bible study HEALED. Jesus pinpointed the problem and removed it in an instant. I want my faith active and available, if Jesus decides to heal my husband.

Satan's Attack: Letting fear rule

Job does not give in to **FEAR** when his health condition changes. He uses the secrets found in God's Word for dealing with things he doesn't understand and can't seem to change. *"He will not fear evil tidings; his heart is steadfast, **trusting in the Lord**." Psalm 112:7 "My times are in Thy hand." Psalm 31:15a* One thing we can always do in physical trials, we can look ahead **to the eternal bodies we will someday enjoy**: *"For you have been born again not of seed which is **perishable but imperishable**."* I Peter 1:23 *"Therefore, since we receive a kingdom **which cannot be shaken**..."* Hebrews 12:2

Satan's Attack: Piercing relationships with pain

Satan tries to dishearten Job by **piercing key relationships with pain**. If Satan senses that the opinions of others are more important to us than God's, he will saturate our lives with attacks in this area.

"My brothers have acted deceitfully like a wadi, like the torrents of wadis which vanish." Job 6:15 *"Then his wife said to him, 'Do you still hold fast your integrity? Curse God and die!'"* Job 2:9

The Apostle Paul reminds us, in Galatians 1:10, that if we are still seeking the favor of men, we cannot be Christ's servants. If you are a people-pleaser the enemy will try this attack continually.

Satan's Attack: Smear your reputation

Over the years, the Lord has brought many families to our church. That has been a wonderful blessing. But over time, there have been many families who have "left our church." The circumstances have varied, but as any pastor knows, sometimes these incidents are heart-wrenching. When others have said wrongful things and caused others to leave, it has hurt our hearts. Our first reaction is to want to defend our positions. However, pastors can't always share the knowledge behind a decision without hurting someone or revealing information they do not have permission to share. It is hard to trust the Lord when someone is saying things that strike at the very root of your character, but to be effective in prayer you will have to allow the enemy to muddy up your reputation from time to time. When he sees that your reputation, as well as your life, is on the altar, and that it is not a hot button that causes you to reel and react, he will move on to test you in new territory. He only uses tactics that work.

An interesting note: One gentleman who caused several families to leave our church, early on, came in and apologized to my husband years later for all the trouble he had stirred up. When I heard he had done this my unspoken thought was, "Would you mind if we published that in the bulletin?" (Smile.) Alas, it was just a precious gift from the Lord. He tells us that He sees in secret the right decisions we make by submitting our will in prayer and rewards us the same way. *"But you, when you pray, go into your inner room, and when you have shut your door, pray to your Father who is in secret, and your Father who sees in secret will repay you." Matthew 6:6*

Satan's Attack:
Get your own "good" without waiting on God

Satan tries to encourage us to **seek our own "good."** Satan whispers that there is no good in our lives. He tempts us to seek comfort away from God, but God's Word answers back: *"'Woe to the rebellious children,' declares the Lord, 'Who execute a plan, but not Mine, and make an alliance, but not of My Spirit, in order to add sin to sin.'" Isaiah 30:1 "I said to the Lord, 'Thou art my Lord; I have no good besides Thee.'" Psalm 16:2 "And it shall be a tassel for you to look at and remember all the commandments of the Lord, so as to do them and **not follow after your own heart and your own eyes**, after which you played* *the harlot." Numbers 15:39*

Satan's Attack: God doesn't really care

The devil will try to get us off course with the thought that **God's goal is not to help you, but to break you**. The thought comes to Job, in Job 7:17-18, that God is not as concerned with man for man's benefit, but for the pleasure of "trying" him. Job starts thinking, "I am God's target." (7:20, 16:12b-14). The truth is this: God is really for him. He praises Job's faithfulness. But the enemy wants Job to think that God has afflicted him. Reality is that Satan has afflicted him. He wants Job to believe that God is cruel. The truth is found in *Isaiah 30:1: "Therefore the Lord longs to be gracious to you, and therefore He waits on high to have compassion on you. For the Lord is a God of justice; how blessed are all those who long for Him."*

*"But let all who take refuge in Thee be glad, let them ever sing for joy; and mayest Thou shelter them, that those who love Thy name may exult in Thee. For it is Thou who dost bless the righteous man, O Lord, Thou dost surround him with favor as with a shield." Psalm 5:11-12 "And when the Lord raised up judges for them, the Lord was with the judge and delivered them from the hand of their enemies all the days of the judge; for the Lord was **moved to pity by their groaning because of those who oppressed and afflicted them**." Judges 2:1*

Satan's Attack: The bad guy always wins

The deceiver will divert us with the thought that **the sinner always prospers**. Asaph battles this along his spiritual journey. We fight this attack with truth: the sinner may appear to be ahead, but the righteous will prosper in eternity.

*"For I was envious of the arrogant, as **I saw the prosperity of the wicked**. Until I came into the sanctuary of God; then I **perceived their end**. 'Surely Thou dost set them in slippery places; Thou dost cast them down to destruction.' How they are **destroyed in a moment**! They are utterly swept away by sudden terrors!" Psalm 73:3, 17-19 "Do not fret because of evildoers, be not envious toward wrongdoers. For they will **wither quickly** like the grass, and **fade like the green herb**. Rest in the Lord and wait patiently for Him; do not fret because of him who prospers in his way, because of the man who carries out wicked schemes. For evildoers will be cut off, but those who wait for the Lord, they **will inherit the land**. Yet a little while and the wicked man will **be no more**; and you will look carefully for his place, and **he will not be there**. The wicked plots against the righteous, and gnashes at him with his teeth. The Lord laughs at him; for **He sees his day is coming**. The Lord knows the days of the blameless; and their inheritance will be **forever**. But the wicked will perish; and the enemies of the Lord will be like the glory of the pastures, they vanish— like smoke they vanish away. Depart from evil, and do good, so you will abide **forever**. For the Lord loves justice, and does not forsake His godly ones; they are preserved **forever**; but the descendants of the wicked will be cut off. The righteous will inherit the land, and **dwell in it forever**. Psalm 37:1-2, 7, 9-10, 12-13, 18, 20, 27-29*

We can watch Job wade through the mire and muck of *half* truth. The spiritual battle comes in dividing truth from falsehood. Both Job and his friends speak some truth and some misinformation. God's Word is what rightly divides it all.

"'No weapon that is formed against you shall prosper; and every tongue that accuses you in judgment you will condemn. This is the heritage of the servants of the Lord, and

their vindication is from Me.' declares the Lord." Isaiah 54:17

When you are on the side of God's purposes you cannot lose

"I know that Thou canst do all things, and that no purpose of Thine can be thwarted." Job 42:2 "Devise a plan but it will be thwarted; state a proposal, but it will not stand, for God is with us." Isaiah 8:10

There is no similarity in the battle plans God has Israel employ in warfare. Sometimes they were to go out and attack. Other times they were to stand still. Once, their offensive strategy was to sing. Another time they were to be silent. But one thing stayed the same, no matter what battle we are talking about, as long as the Israelites followed God's instructions, they never lost. They were always on the winning side. Some battles were quickly concluded in a matter of hours. Some campaigns went on for years (as when they took over the Promised Land). I'm not sure what battles you or I will face in the future, but I do know this, that with God laying out the strategy for our lives and with us being obedient, we will not lose.

11

Exercising Humility in Prayer

Humility is another powerful tool we need to use if we will be used greatly by God in prayer. It is not a lesson we will learn once, but one that we will have to practice every day of our lives. It is so easy for Satan to tempt us into thinking we are something apart from God. No matter how long you have walked with God, you are only a millisecond away from a prideful thought. The more you pray, the more God uses you, and the greater the temptation to think you had something to do with it. WRONG! As my husband frequently says from the pulpit: "You are clay pipe—just a conduit through which God works." I was profoundly affected through the reading of Andrew Murray's book on humility and this led me to search the Scriptures and to recognize my need for more of it in my life.

God points out our need for humility with irony

There was a night that I was scheduled to teach a class on humility at our church. I crack up just remembering the irony of the situation. At the last minute, our children's ministry needed someone to fill in. I struggled for a while over the decision because I thought, "I can't, I'm the BIG Bible study teacher. I've got to teach on humility." How I must have made God laugh! A friend suggested that maybe I postpone my class a week and help out with the need. For me the hardest time to be humble is when someone expects it. It's easy to be a servant when you've determined you want to be, but it's hard when someone else decides you should be a servant (and treats you like one.) Finally, I submitted my will, postponed the Bible study and helped the children. God didn't just want me to teach about humility. He wanted me to LEARN it!

Then the following week my children got sick. I was a little in a huff because I was dying to teach this lesson on humility. God used this to point out my need again. Humility is understanding that you are not the center of the universe. Humility is laying aside your own desires and dreams to be God's servant and there is no time off-duty. So again, the class was postponed while I worked on my *homework* of helping to care for my children and their needs above my own

Three weeks later I finally got to teach the class. I taught from a vantagepoint of greater effectiveness because God had been teaching me what it was all about. Lest you think that I believe I have arrived in this area, let me inform you of the contrary. Just a couple of weeks ago, I got my nose out of joint over some silly change to a song in our worship rehearsal. God had to send our friend, Rev. Al Howard, to preach a message entitled "Getting the Stallion Out," and used it to show me the root of my frustration: pride. How God hates it! How it messes up His work! Again, that day I submitted to God's work of producing humility in my life.

Humility is just internalizing the reality of our condition.

Humility is really just discovering who you are in Christ. At your best, you are simply called to be a **bond servant**. As we mature in Christ, we realize more and more that we are less and less. We do not come out of the womb with this attitude. The work of God allows us to recognize it and live out its truth. **Humility is also purposefully promoting the reality of our condition to others**. It's recognizing the truth of the next two verses: *"Truly, truly, I say to you, **a slave is not greater than his master;** neither is one who is sent greater than the one who sent him."* John 13:16 *"**Is the ax to boast itself over the one who chops with it?** Is the saw to exalt itself over the one who wields it? That would be like a club wielding those who lift it, or like a rod lifting him who is not wood."* Isaiah 10:15 We are the club or ax in the analogy. God is the one who lifts us and uses us. How can we boast in the wood that is chopped? What is an ax without the hand that lifts it?

During the time when I was recuperating from emotional hurt, there were many ministry tasks I was not capable of being a part of. My involvement in church activities had been pared back from ten to four. One delicious truth that God taught me during this time was that He didn't need my help to hold up the world. That might seem humorous, but I can't say I really knew it before this time. Once I could grasp that the world and our church could run successfully without my help, I was a happier me. No longer did I have to do things just because they wouldn't get done any other way. This is a painfully honest picture of my pride, but one I had to face. Once I understood that God didn't NEED me to accomplish His work, I had only learned half the lesson.

Months went by, watching others lead ministries, and we saw tremendous growth in many areas, but there was still something missing. It seems God always uses cooking pictures to teach me. Smile.

You are my bay leaf

"You are the bay leaf in my *body of Christ stew,*" He said to my heart. "You are not the meat and the potatoes. That's My role. I sustain life. I bring the nutrients. But I allow you, my creation, to bring flavor to MY pot." Have you ever eaten stew cooked without a bay leaf? Something is missing. God tried to teach me that my life could add a touch of spice to the body of Christ that no one else could add. It would be my choice to be used by His hand to bring a full flavor or not. If more Christians could learn this lesson, then the church would be what God intended it to be. Every gift, every personality, every passion, sprinkled over His work, would find us all going home fed and full.

This is a hard lesson to learn, but a helpful one. It's not easy to be prideful when you realize you're just a bay leaf. But this picture is going to help me fight Satan when he tries to tell me I don't have a necessary place in God's house.

God wants to use you

I love this little story and its truth can bring comfort when our "person" is under attack.

"A story is told of a king who went into his garden one morning, and found everything withered and dying. He asked the oak that stood near the gate what the trouble was. He found it was sick of life and determined to die because it was not tall and beautiful like the pine. The pine was all out of heart because if could not bear grapes, like the vine. The vine

was going to throw its life away because it could not stand erect and have as fine a fruit as the peach tree. The geranium was fretting because it was not tall and fragrant like the lilac; and so on all through the garden. Coming to a heartsease, he found its bright face lifted as cheery as ever. "Well, heartsease, I'm glad, amidst all this discouragement to find one brave little flower. You do not seem to be the least disheartened." "No, I am not of much account, but I thought that if you wanted an oak, or a pine, or a peach tree, or a lilac, you would have planted one, but as I knew you wanted a heartsease, I am determined to be the best little heartsease that I can." Mrs. Charles E. Cowman, <u>Streams in the Desert</u>, p. 14.

It's much easier to complete our servant job when we have an accurate description of what is expected. A servant is expected to lay aside his own priorities and desires to serve the master with His needs and desires.

Look at these Bible heroes
who had learned this life lesson:

Moses – *"Now the man Moses was **very humble, more than any man who was on the face of the earth**." Numbers 12:3* He thought he was somebody for 40 years. Then he learned over the next 40 years that he was nobody. Then he was finally somebody God could use for the next 40 years. *"Remember the law of Moses **My servant**." Malachi 4:4a "Now Moses was faithful in all His house **as a servant**, for a testimony of those things which were to be spoken later." Hebrews 3:5 "And they sang the song of Moses the **bondservant** of God and the song of the Lamb, saying, 'Great and marvelous are Thy works, O Lord God, the Almighty; righteous and true are Thy ways, Thou King of the nations.'" Revelation 15:3 "But Moses said to God, '**Who am I**, that I should go to Pharaoh, and that I should bring the sons of*

Israel out of Egypt?' " *Exodus 3:11*

Joseph – We see a big difference in the Joseph who proudly asserts his dreaming abilities and the one who bows before the only One able to give a dream and its interpretation. *"And he said to them, 'Please listen to this dream which I have had.'* " *Genesis 37:6 "Now he had still another dream, and related it to his brothers, and said, 'Lo, I have had still another dream; and behold, the sun and the moon and eleven stars were bowing down to me.'* " *Genesis 37:9 "Joseph then answered Pharaoh, saying, 'It is not in me; God will give Pharaoh a favorable answer.'* " *Genesis 41:16*

David – *"Then David the king went in and sat before the Lord and said,* **Who am I***, O Lord God, and what is my house that Thou hast brought me this far?'* " *I Chronicles 17:16 "O Lord,* **my heart is not proud***, nor my eyes haughty; nor do I involve myself in great matters, or in things too difficult for me." Psalm 131:1 "And has raised up a horn of salvation for us in the house of David* **His servant***." Luke 1:69 "Who by the Holy Spirit, through the mouth of our father* **David Thy servant***, didst say, 'Why did the Gentiles rage, And the peoples devise futile things?'* " *Acts 4:25*

Jesus – *"But emptied Himself, taking the form of a* **bond-servant***, and being made in the likeness of men..." Philippians 2:7 "Behold,* **My Servant** *whom I have chosen..." Matthew 12:1a "The God of Abraham, Isaac, and Jacob, the God of our fathers, has glorified* **His servant Jesus***, the one whom you delivered up, and disowned in the presence of Pilate, when he had decided to release Him." Acts 3:1 3 "For you first, God raised up* **His Servant***, and sent Him to bless you by turning every one of you from your wicked ways." Acts 3:26 "For truly in this city there were gathered together against* **Thy holy servant Jesus***, whom*

*Thou didst anoint, both Herod and Pontius Pilate, along with the Gentiles and the peoples of Israel." Acts 4:27 "While Thou dost extend Thy hand to heal, and signs and wonders take place through the name of **Thy holy servant Jesus**." Acts 4:30* **Jesus' message was to take your own pride "down, down, down" so God could raise you "up, up, up."** *"It is not so among you, but whoever wishes to become great among you shall be your servant." Matthew 20:26 "But the greatest among you shall be your servant." Matthew 23:11 "And sitting down, He called the twelve and said to them, 'If anyone wants to be first, he shall be last of all, and servant of all.' " Mark 9:35 "But not so with you, but let him who is the greatest among you become as the youngest, and the leader as the servant." Luke 22:26 "If anyone serves Me, let him follow Me; and where I am, there shall My servant also be; if anyone serves Me, the Father will honor him." John 12:26*

"Christ's triumph was in His humiliation. Possibly our triumph also, is to be made manifest in what seems to others humiliation." Margaret Bottome, (Quoted by Mrs. Charles Cowman), <u>Streams in the Desert</u>*, p. 114.*

Paul – *"Paul, a **bond-servant** of Christ Jesus, called as an apostle, set apart for the gospel of God." Romans 1:1 "For am I now seeking the favor of men, or of God? Or am I striving to please men? If I were still trying to please men, I would not be a **bond-servant** of Christ." Galatians 1:10 "Paul and Timothy, **bond-servants** of Christ Jesus, to all the saints in Christ Jesus who are in Philippi, including the overseers and deacons." Philippians 1:1 "Paul, a **bond-servant** of God, and an apostle of Jesus Christ, for the faith of those chosen of God and the knowledge of the truth which is according to godliness..." Titus 1:1 "What then is Apollos? And what is Paul? **Servants** through whom you believed,* *even as the Lord gave opportunity to each one." I Corinthians 3:5 "Are they **servants** of Christ? I speak as if insane. I more so; in far more labors, in far more imprisonments, beaten times without number, often in danger of death." I Corinthians 3:5 "Let a man regard us in this manner, **as servants of Christ**, and stewards of the mysteries of God." I Corinthians 4:1 "Who also made us adequate as **servants of a new covenant**, not of the letter, but of the Spirit; for the letter kills, but the Spirit gives life." II Corinthians 3:6 "But in everything commending ourselves as **servants of God**, in much endurance, in afflictions, in hardships, in distresses..." II Corinthians 6:4 "I have become foolish; you yourselves compelled me. Actually I should have been commended by you, for in no respect was I inferior to the most eminent apostles, **even though I am a nobody**." II Corinthians 12:11*

Solomon – *"And now, O Lord my God, Thou hast made Thy servant king in place of my father David, yet **I am but a little child; I do not know how to go out or come in**." I Kings 3:7 "Wisdom and knowledge have been granted to you. And I will give you riches and wealth and honor, such as none of the kings who were before you has possessed, nor those who will come after you." II Chronicles 1:12*

John the Baptist - *"He must increase, but I must decrease." John 3:30 "As for me, I baptize you with water for repentance, but He who is coming after me is mightier than I, and I am not fit to remove His sandals; He will baptize you with the Holy Spirit and fire." Matthew 3:11 "But John tried to prevent Him, saying, 'I have need to be baptized by You, and do You come to me?' " Matthew 3:14*

The Phoenician woman - *"And He was saying to her, 'Let the children be satisfied first, for it is not good to take the* *children's bread and throw it to the dogs.' But she answered and said to Him, 'Yes, Lord, but even the dogs under the table feed on the children's crumbs.'" Mark 7:27-28* (Even the puppies, the little dogs, the insignificant ones…)

Where does all your ability originate?

When we realize that everything we are and are able to do has come from God, it is hard to get puffed up about it. *"But who am I and who are my people that we should be able to offer as generously as this?* **For all things come from Thee, and from Thy hand we have given Thee.**" *I Chronicles 29:14 "For who regards you as superior?* **And what do you have that you did not receive?** *But if you did receive it,* **why do you boast as if you had not received it**?" *I Corinthians 4:7 "***Not that we are adequate in ourselves to consider anything as coming from ourselves***, but our adequacy is from God." II Corinthians 3:5 "But we have this treasure in earthen vessels, that the surpassing greatness of the power* **may be of God and not from ourselves**." *II Corinthians 4:7*

Learning this can be a great blessing. When we understand that all ability comes from God, then we can ask for more. I asked the Lord to empower me to write this book in January 2002. He did it in February 2003. He even gave me the suggestion of adding prayer journal entries on Jan. 27, 2003, during my quiet time. It's a very freeing lesson to learn. When the king asked Daniel to interpret his dream, Daniel was quick to distinguish between his ability and God's ability: He said, "It is not IN ME." In my life also, I see the huge difference in the quality and depth of what the Almighty God is capable of compared to the weakness and limited nature of my own efforts. The good stuff "is not in me."

Abilities are handicaps when they keep me from seeing my utter dependence on Jesus

You were not chosen for what you WERE, but for what you WERE NOT - *I Corinthians 1:27 "But God has chosen the foolish things of the world to shame the wise, and God has chosen the weak things of the world to shame the things which are strong,"*

You are a like a ping pong ball

Sometimes, when I speak, I like to bring along a ping pong ball. "This represents your life," I tell them. "You are small, weak and limited." Sometimes at this point I even squash the ball with my foot. "You may not even live that long. But God the creator of the world says that you and I can make an indelible mark on our world. He says that we can do impossible things through our prayers." At this point in the message, I ask if anyone thinks I can make the ping pong ball hang in the air without anybody touching it. If I'm speaking at a chapel a few little heads bob up and down, but the older grades shake their heads. We go on to discuss the law of gravity and how no matter what I try this ping pong ball is not capable of breaking the laws of the universe.

However, there is a way to make this little, weak, limited ping pong ball hang in the air without any human hands touching it. I remind them that God, who created gravity can tell the laws of the universe to take a hike anytime He wants to. When He tells us that we can do, literally, the impossible, He has the power to make it happen. Then I pull out a hairdryer and turn it on under the ball. Without fail the little ball hangs in the air without the aid of human hands. When the light bulb inside our own heads goes on and we realize that everything we need to know or change about our world comes under the heading of God's abilities, then we realize that it is a delightful opportunity to be His ping pong ball. The weaker we are, the better. The less capable we are in our abilities, the greater it will be for His glory.

I have to remember this often when God calls on me to teach. As many others God has used throughout the centuries, I am painfully aware of my own weaknesses in public speaking. However God's lesson to Moses on the subject has not failed to catch my eye and I have to read it often to remind myself that God loves using ping pong balls like me for this very reason.

"Then Moses said to the Lord, 'Please, Lord, I have never been eloquent, neither recently nor in time past, nor since Thou hast spoken to Thy servant; for I am slow of speech and slow of tongue.' And the Lord said to him, 'Who has made man's mouth? Or who makes him dumb or deaf, or seeing or blind? Is it not I, the Lord? **Now then go, and I, even I, will be with your mouth, and teach you what you are to say.'** *"* Exodus 4:10-12

What can you accomplish that is lasting apart from Him?

The centuries are littered with monuments to man's frailty and transient life span. Decaying statues and civilizations remind us that the only thing we can build that will last must be in connection with Jesus Christ.

*"And let the rich man glory in his **humiliation**, because like flowering grass he will pass away."* James 1:10 *"I am the vine, you are the branches; he who abides in Me, and I in him, he bears much fruit;* **for apart from Me you can do nothing**.*"* John 15:5 *"As for the days of our life, they contain seventy years, or if due to strength, eighty years,* **yet**

their pride is but labor and sorrow; for soon it is gone and we fly away." Psalm 90:10

What have you done that deserves praise?

*"But which of you, having a slave plowing or tending sheep, will say to him when he has come in from the field, 'Come immediately and sit down to eat'? But will he not say to him, 'Prepare something for me to eat, and properly clothe yourself and serve me until I have eaten and drunk; and afterward you will eat and drink'? He does not thank the slave because he did the things which were commanded, does he? So you too, when you do all the things which are commanded you, say, **'We are unworthy slaves; we have done only that which we ought to have done.'** " Luke 17:7-10*

This scripture sums it up pretty well. When we do what Jesus asks us to, we are simply doing our job. There is no need to blow the trumpets and hand out certificates. When servants serve it doesn't make the front-page news. That's what servants are supposed to do. It's when those who should be servants, do not act like servants, that the world takes notice. It's usually then that the church appears on the front page of the news.

How you view yourself will determine how you treat others.

Like servanthood, the hardest time to be humble is when others are treating you as if you are less important. We display our true attitude about ourselves in how we react when people waste our time and ideas. This does not mean that, to be truly humble, we are to allow the waste of these things. They are only thermometers that can reveal the temperature of the problem. The root is not our reaction.

The root is the attitude that ends up in a reaction.

"*Be of the same mind toward one another;* **do not be haughty in mind**, *but associate with the lowly.* **Do not be wise in your own estimation**." Romans 12:16 "*The fear of the Lord is to* **hate evil; pride and arrogance and the evil way**, *and the perverted mouth, I hate.*" Proverbs 8:13

"*It is easy to think we humble ourselves before God;* **humility towards men will be the only sufficient proof that our humility before God is real**; *that humility has taken up its abode in us, and become our very nature; that we actually, like Christ, have made ourselves of no reputation.*" Andrew Murray, Humility, p. 44.

Humility becomes a tool
that empowers us to live in unity

Jesus understood that more humility in the lives of His disciples, would affect their conversation, *(Who gets to sit at your right hand, Jesus?")*, their friendships, *("Greater love has no one than this, that one lay down his life for his friends." John 15:13)*, and their concern for the unsaved *(Moses, who was the more humble man who ever lived said in Exodus 32:32 "But now, if Thou wilt, forgive their sin—and if not, please blot me out from Thy book which Thou hast written!")*.

Jesus also knows that more humility in our lives will cool our tempers, increase our effectiveness in ministry and drive the enemy crazy! "*Wives, be subject to your husbands, as is fitting in the Lord.*" Colossians 3:1 "*Do nothing from selfishness or empty conceit, but with humility of mind let each of you regard one another as more important than himself.*" Philippians 2:3 "*Servants, be submissive to your masters with all respect, not only to those who are good and gentle, but also to those who are unreasonable." I Peter 2:1*

Life Tool: Disarm the enemy with the attitude of humility. *YOU BE THE QUEEN!*

I'm sure men don't struggle with this issue as much as women do. There is this thing that happens when two women walk into the kitchen together, or meet to share about their lives. A subtle competitive feeling starts making its way into the conversation. One woman will share that her child made honor roll. The other responds that her child has made honor roll every year. It's a deadly, stealth-like, form of sin. I had noticed this happening with one of my friends and recognized how much it hurt my heavenly Father, so the next time we were together, I decided to make a change. The change began in my heart. I decided right off to think this thought: "You be the queen." In other words, I saw the other person in the place of honor and me in the role of the humble servant. This imperceptible change of attitude in me affected the course of the entire encounter and now I use it frequently whenever I feel pride huffing its way into my head.

"Let us look upon every brother who tries or vexes us, as God's means of grace, God's instrument for our purification, for our exercises of the humility Jesus our LIFE breathes within us." Andrew Murray, <u>Humility</u>, p. 51

"A faithful servant may be wiser than the master; and yet retain the true Spirit and posture of the servant." Andrew Murray, <u>Humility</u>, p. 47 (This is how the servants of Nabal, the fool, acted after being given his ridiculous orders.)

The highest place of spiritual maturity is the lowest state of "self"

The farther we want to go with God, the lower we will have to go in service. What I mean is this: God can't use you to do great things until He knows He can count on you to do little and sometimes seemingly insignificant things.

Everyone likes to think he is mature. As Christians, we desire to attain to Christ-likeness, or spiritual maturity. But how do we assess our progress? In what ways can we truly determine the stature of our inner man?

Andrew Murray, in his book **Humility**, puts it this way: *"What a solemn thought, that our love to God will be measured by our everyday intercourse with men and the love it displays; and that our love to God will be found to be a delusion, except as its truth is proved in standing the test of daily life with our fellow-men."*

"Folly is set in many exalted places while rich men sit in **humble places***."* Ecclesiastes 10:6 *"But let the brother of* **humble** *circumstances glory in his* **high position***;"* James 1:9 *"Whoever then* **humbles himself as this child***, he is the greatest in the kingdom of heaven."* Matthew 1:4

Learning the lesson of genuine humility becomes the door to God's blessing.

Until we learn the lesson of humility, honor will only be a detriment or distraction to our spiritual progress. Joseph sat in prison year after year until he was no longer a dreamer of self. When God saw that he was emptied of *selfish ambition* then He could open the door of influence and blessing. Now God knew that what was meant for blessing would not become a curse to Joseph's spiritual development.

Meditate on these verses in your prayer time today:
"You younger men, likewise, be subject to your elders; and all of you, **clothe yourselves with humility toward one another,** *for God is opposed to the proud,* **but gives grace to the humble. Humble yourselves, therefore,** *under the mighty hand of God,* **that He may exalt you at the proper time.***" I Peter 5:5-6 "The fear of the Lord is the instruction for wisdom,* **and before honor comes humility.***" Proverbs 15:33 "A man's pride will bring him low,* **but a humble spirit will obtain honor.***" Proverbs 29:23 "He has brought down rulers from their thrones,* **and has exalted those who were humble.***" Luke 1:52 "The reward of humility and the fear of the Lord* **are riches, honor and life.***" Proverbs 22:4*

**The lesson of genuine humility
becomes the door to real learning.**

Have you ever tried to teach someone something that they think they already know? I made a suggestion one time to a young couple about the way they were handling their toddler. (I'm such an expert on such things!) I could see right away that they couldn't really hear a word I was saying, because they thought they ALREADY knew the right thing to do. Humility reveals itself in the acceptance of instruction. Pride turns away from correction.

When I think of how much I used to think I knew, it blows my mind. I would skip into a convention workshop and after five minutes, if I didn't think the instructor knew enough, I would slip out. The audacity of that kind of thinking! I still struggle with that attitude from time to time. But I have seen the face of my Savior and how my pride affects His countenance. I have, like Job, prayed from an ash heap (symbolic) and realized that everything in my life has been a gift from God. The sin of pride now stinks like a rotten banana when I find it stuffed into the backpack of my thinking.

*"A poor, yet wise lad is better than an old and foolish king **who no longer knows how to receive instruction**." Ecclesiastes 4:13 "The way of a fool is right in his own eyes, **but a wise man is he who listens to counsel**." Proverbs 12:15 "**He who trusts in his own heart is a fool**, but he who walks wisely will be delivered." Proverbs 2:26 "Who is this that hides counsel without knowledge? Therefore I have declared that which I did not understand, things too wonderful for me, which I did not know." Job 42:3*

As incredible as it seems, learning the lesson of genuine humility leads to power and influence. Listen to this story by Dr. Bill Bright about a friend's experience:

"A dear friend, Dee Jepsen, wife of former U.S. Senator Roger Jepsen, attended a luncheon in the Senate Caucus Room on Capitol Hill in Washington, DC. Congressmen, Cabinet members, top leaders in government, and many other respected guests were seated in the impressive room with its ornate pillars, high ceilings, and huge chandeliers. The room seemed to swell with influential people who had gathered to honor a humble servant of God. Then Mother Teresa entered the room. Mrs. Jepsen said, 'She looked so tiny and out-of-place in her blue-and-white habit, old gray sweater, and sandals that had obviously carried her many miles. The room and prestigious guests seemed to dwarf her.' Immediately the top leaders of the most powerful country in the world along with the other esteemed guests rose to their feet and applauded. Many had tears in their eyes. 'I was struck with the contrast,' Mrs. Jepsen said. 'I thought, Lord, this frail woman has more power than I see in the Halls of Congress. She reflects Jesus everywhere she goes, and everyone is strangely moved.' Mother Teresa doesn't own anything; she has never asked for material possessions nor held up her fist to demand rights for herself. Yet she has been

raised to a pinnacle of recognition for her work with the destitute and dying in Calcutta, India. She has reached down into the gutter and loved those whom the world has called unlovable. A shining example of selflessness, she proves the power of God's love to transform people and touch a starved world. This is real power and, unlike that of the world, it confounds the wise and humbles the mighty. It is the power of God working through ordinary men and women for His glory. Our Lord, God in the flesh, was an example of sheer, unlimited power, but controlled and restrained for His mission, and driven by love. When we are filled with His Spirit, we have that same power inside of us. But He wants us to be vessels of His mission, **to walk in His humility**, and also to be driven by His love. Then people will not see us, but will see Him in us. Like Mother Teresa, we will display a power the world does not know. But His Spirit working in us will draw others to Himself."* Written in an email newsletter by Dr. Bill Bright, Founder of Campus Crusade*

Humility is a trait of our father

Pride is the mark of our former slave master. Humility is the mark of our Father. The more we walk in an emptied state of existence, the more God can anoint us with fresh power. *"For all that is in the world, the lust of the flesh and the lust of the eyes and the boastful pride of life, **is not from the Father, but is from the world.**" I John 2:16*

"Humility, the place of entire dependence on God, is, from the very nature of things, the first duty and the highest virtue of the creature, and the root of every virtue. And so pride, or the loss of this humility, is the root of every sin and evil." Andrew Murray, <u>Humility</u>, p. 12

Whatever experience God uses to teach humility becomes a blessing.

The children of Israel must have hated the wilderness. (I hate living out of a suitcase for even a week.) But God was going to use rocks, manna and quail to teach His people to quit relying on themselves and to seek His power and authority. *"And you shall remember all the way which the Lord your God has led you in the wilderness these forty years,* **that He might humble you***, testing you, to know what was in your heart, whether you would keep His commandments or not." Deuteronomy 8:2* *"In the wilderness He fed you manna which your fathers did not know,* **that He might humble you** *and that He might test you, to do good for you in the end." Deuteronomy 8:16*Whatever painful experiences you have endured can achieve the same result. You can find a treasure chest of power in understanding how utterly helpless you really are.

"Therefore I am well content with weaknesses, with insults, with distresses, with persecutions, with difficulties, for Christ's sake; for when I am weak, then I am strong." II Corinthians 12:10

— 12 —

Learning to Fear the Lord in Prayer

When we realize that God can teach us what to say, what to do, where to go, etc., then the possibilities for our lives become unlimited. When we understand that He is the power source and we are simply the vehicles, then we are ready to be useful in prayer. This is what it means to learn to "fear the Lord." When we get deeply under our skin that God can do anything, then in response we find that we can do ANYTHING in His power. God's Word tells us this is actually the first lesson we must learn in order to learn everything else God wants to teach us. But I have placed it at the end of the book because it is not a lesson we learn once. We will learn it every time we face a new obstacle and trust God to overcome it. Learning to fear the Lord will require a lifetime of homework.

This principle is such an important one for prayer that we must spend a little time here. The more we learn about God's authority, the more we can become audacious in our asking. The disciples were on a three-year journey of learning what God had authority over. They learned, through each day's encounter, that He had authority over sickness, demons, sin, weather, resources, their own weakness, and finally over death itself. They had to endure a raging sea so that they could learn that God has authority over storms. They had to face the five thousand with five rolls so that they could learn that God has authority over daily bread. Peter had to draw up a fish with a coin in its mouth so he could learn that God has authority over the fish of the sea, and his tax bill as well.

Lifetimes are lessons in learning about the authority of God. The more we know, the more we can respond with belief and obedience. As God introduces more of Himself, we see that there is more to marvel at. This produces the natural effect of trust and becomes the springboard for prayer.

One year, our family had a two-week vacation coming. We were looking forward to the rest, but finances were tight. I believed God had authority over finances, circumstances and our lives and so I asked the Lord to use His authority to provide just the vacation activity as well as inactivity that we needed. I was amazed by how He supplied the necessary resources every couple of days. When God knew we needed to go out and have fun the resources came. (God even went so far as to have my cousins leave a special vacation gift and then have us not find it until the very day we needed it.) He had my husband win a contest that provided tickets to a fun-family event. But God also saw that we needed to spend time around the house. There were days no resources came and that was our signal that God wanted us to rest.

There is nothing God can ever ask you to do that he, the Almighty Powerful Hair Dryer (as in the ping pong ball illustration), can't accomplish through you. His ultra wattage is beyond our comprehension. After all, He suspends our world, not just us, in the air with no human hands. You can trust Him. Read these verses and allow God's Word to expand the territory of your trust.

Respect the authority of God over physical strength and resources

"'With him is only an arm of flesh, but with us is the Lord our God to help us and to fight our battles' and the people relied on the words of Hezekiah king of Judah." II Chronicles 32:8 "I will not be afraid of ten thousands of people who have set themselves against me round about." Psalm 3:6 "Though a host encamp against me, my heart will not fear; though war arise against me, in spite of this I shall be confident." Psalm 27:3 "A horse is a false hope for victory; nor does it deliver anyone by its great strength." Psalm 33:17 "For I will not trust in my bow, nor will my sword save me." Psalm 44:6

In the summer of 1979, I felt the Lord tug on my heart to answer the call to do short term missions work in Brazil. I had completed college and the first year of my teaching. (Even the mission field looked good after teaching seventh grade.) As the time approached to "turn in the money" I realized that without God's help this entire trip would be impossible. After weeks and months of praying and waiting, nothing had come in for my trip. I had no money of my own that could pay for the trip.

One night as I lay on my bed, the Lord planted an idea in my head. "Why don't you sell some of the nice antiques you have to pay for the trip?" It sounded to me more like the voice of Satan talking. My parents had given me a few pieces of furniture to decorate an old house my roommate and I had restored for an entire year. I had painstakingly stripped and refinished a few garage sale items to go along with the other things. These simple pieces of furniture were so pretty in a house that had original solid oak bathroom fixtures, high ceilings with picture moldings and brass door fixtures. There was a struggle as I thought about how much work they represented. On the other hand, what good would furniture do me if I was not obedient to the will of God. Late that night, I surrendered them for His use. The next morning my father announced in church that anyone wanting to help with my missions trip could purchase some antiques and thereby help my trip along.

After the service, a retired pastor slipped a check for one hundred dollars into my hand. I knew it was a huge amount for him and his wife who lived on a small pension. Then later, a successful businessman handed me a check for one thousand dollars. This completely covered the entire trip. He told me with a smile, "I don't want your furniture." This was how a very special season in my life began. There is never a yielding without a blessing. There is never a sacrifice for obedience that God doesn't take into account and reward later. But that was only one time to trust God for resources. A more challenging trial came as I was preparing to leave on the trip.

As I sat in church the Sunday I was to depart for Florida to join other team members I heard the voice of God speaking through a sermon my father gave on Malachi chapter 3. Verses 8-10 were his text for the day and the Holy Spirit was drilling the message into my heart: *"Will a man rob God? Yet you are robbing Me! But you say, 'How have we robbed Thee?' In tithes and offerings. You are cursed with a curse, for you are robbing Me, the whole nation of you!* "*Bring the whole tithe into the storehouse, so that there may be food in My house, and test Me now in this," says the Lord of hosts, "if I will not open for you the windows of heaven, and pour out for you a blessing until it overflows."* I am a creative person, not a detail person. And as I sat through this message I realized that I had forgotten to pay my tithe. As I added up what was due the Lord, I realized it was seventy dollars. That was a horrible thought to have, as you are about to travel thousands of miles away to do ministry work. The day before I had gotten traveler's checks for spending money. I would be gone for six weeks. I bet you can guess how much money I had? That's right, I had seventy dollars. Another struggle for complete Lordship went on in the few minutes that remained of the message. I knew what I must do. God could never bless my trip if I ignored what He had already told me to do. I quietly turned each check over, signed it and placed it in the offering plate. I was careful to make sure no one saw me doing this.

As I left the sanctuary to leave for the airport a precious elderly saint pressed an envelope into my hand. Later on the plane I found it contained a five-dollar bill. As we had driven to the airport, my father had asked me if I had enough money for the trip. I didn't want to lie. Nor did I want to tell him that I had left my traveler's checks in the offering. He would have just re-filled my purse and I wanted to hold the Lord to his promise of a blessing. Very carefully I chose words that were truthful. "You were with me yesterday at the bank," I said. "You saw me get those checks." He nodded. Then he handed me a ten-dollar bill. I want you to put this in your wallet. If you don't need it, you can give it back to me after the trip is over. (He and I both somehow knew he'd never see that ten spot again.)

It didn't take but a week to see that fifteen dollars gone. With long layovers in airports, a Pepsi here or there, film to buy, etc. the money was soon gone. There were five weeks left through which I would have to trust the Lord to provide the resources I needed.

Several challenges came along during that trip that

would make me lean all my weight on the promise God had made to bless me with a blessing that could not be contained. First, after walking many miles a day doing evangelism, my shoes began to wear out. The toes of both shoes began to "flap" as I walked. We were ministering to the poor and I soon began to look more and more like one of them. Then my purse strap broke. I tied it into a knot and continued to serve. There were many times when someone on the team wanted to buy a Coke or a candy bar for refreshment. Out of the bus would pour twenty or so young people. They would stream into a little village market and come out eating and drinking. These were times of fasting for me. I would sit alone with the Lord and remind Him that I had obeyed His Word. I would tell Him that I was waiting to see His blessing.

Usually my teammate and I stayed in a very lovely home. Our host family was well to do and we enjoyed all the comforts of home plus fresh baked bread and hot chocolate each day. But one night we traveled out to the village and were required to stay in a very poor home. The meal that night was unforgettable. Meat was not often enjoyed by the poorest of Brazilian families and so the fact that they offered it to us was meaningful. However, earlier in the day we had toured the nearby market and saw the dogs that freely ran up to the fresh meat, taking all the free licks that they wanted. I knew, as I looked at the dinner we were about to eat, that it was very likely this meat had been among what had been licked earlier in the day. The woman of the home had prepared spaghetti with meat. Unfortunately the fat had not been drained and because we were eating later than expected, the fat had hardened on top of the noodles. It was like eating chunks of lard and I almost gagged on every bite. I hate mango punch, but it saved my life that night because every bite was washed down with a slug of it. I wondered, in a complaining way, as I went to sleep, "Why did I have to come here, Lord? Why couldn't I have just stayed with my regular family?"

In the morning, I looked down where I had left my shoes. They had been meticulously mended and polished. I ran out to the father of the family and asked, "Who did this?" He smiled and replied that the elves had come in the night. Later, in my time with God, He spoke to my heart. "I didn't bring you here for what YOU could give THEM. I brought you here for what THEY could give YOU."

I also celebrated my birthday while there. Our regular host family bought me a new leather purse as a present. (God had provided all that I needed.)

One day, when a lot of team members were getting treats I uttered a WISH prayer: "God, I wish I had a chocolate ice cream so bad I can almost taste it." It's best to wish for things that actually exist in the country where you are traveling. I found out as we traveled that Brazilians didn't even have what we call ice cream. They had Italian ices, but they really didn't have anything close to the hard creamy taste we enjoy. Later, that afternoon, we were surprised by a host pastor's words. He told us that their church wanted to treat us to ice cream. Can you guess the flavor? It was chocolate. It was a gel-like consistency and had a different taste, but it was an answer to my prayers. I praised the Lord for every lick!

That trip was pivotal for me. I learned that God could take care of me, without the aid of my gracious father, without automated teller machines, which weren't invented yet, and without traveler's checks. I learned like the disciples, who were sent out without purse or bread or extra coat, that God was able to provide everything I needed to do His will and work. This is an important lesson and one that helped greatly when my husband and I planted a church years later.

Respect the authority of God over the authority of man

"The Lord is for me; I will not fear; what can man do to me?" Psalm 11:6 "But Peter and the apostles answered and said, 'We must obey God rather than men.' " Acts 5:29 "The fear of man brings a snare, but he who trusts in the Lord will be exalted." Proverbs 29:25 "Do not fear them, for the Lord your God is the one fighting for you." Deuteronomy 3:22

The midwives who helped the Israelites save their boy babies had learned this lesson. They did what God *demanded*, not what their government *expected* and God rewarded them with families of their own. Every day in America there are unsung heroes posing as educators, physicians and judges who do the *right thing*. They have learned the truth of Psalm 11:6 in the core of their being. Have you learned this concept? Is there ever something your employer asks you to do that is under-handed? Are you ever encouraged to disobey the teachings of God's Word? Are you told to not speak about your faith, not to pray, and pressured by the fact that you will lose your job if you do? Take a hint from the midwives. When you obey God, He takes on the responsibility for your job security. He may remove you from where you are now, but it's only so He can promote you. (Even being laid off will result in eternal social security and blessing.)

Respect the authority of God over catastrophic news and events

"Therefore we will not fear, though the earth should change, and though the mountains slip into the heart of the sea." Psalm 46:2 "He will not fear evil tidings; his heart is steadfast, trusting in the Lord." Psalm 112:7 "But he who listens to me shall live securely, and shall be at ease from the dread of evil." Proverbs 1:33 "Do not fear what you are

about to suffer. Behold, the devil is about to cast some of you into prison, that you may be tested, and you will have tribulation ten days. Be faithful until death, and I will give you the crown of life." Revelation 2:10

America has never faced such unpredictable times before. In one day, nuclear war could erupt over the mid-east crisis. We can face such turbulence with the knowledge that God is in control. He even shows us through the Word that He can, at one moment in time, bring judgment and in the same circumstances protect His people. Think of how God cared for Noah and his family, while He brought judgment on the whole world. He cared for Lot's family, while two cities were completely destroyed. And He can care for you and me, despite whatever circumstances come our way.

Respect the authority of God over nature:

"And the men marveled, saying, 'What kind of a man is this, that even the winds and the sea obey Him?' " Matthew 8:27

When the ground was being prepared for our current church building, a huge hole was dug for the foundation. Ike, my husband, began asking the people of our church to pray for **NO RAIN** until this phase was completed. Too much rain would fill that hole slowing down the entire construction project and there had already been enough delays. All during that time period we only experienced one light sprinkle that did no damage at all.

Now I am not advocating that we walk outside and command either rain or sun to suit our plans, but I am very definitely encouraging us to know that there is a time to exert authority over weather. Elijah knew that as long as the grass was green and the gardens were bearing that his country was going to continue to go down the tubes. No rain was a way to wake them up to the spiritual reality of their condition. He was a man of like nature to us. He prayed and normal rainfall was withheld. Then the contest on Mt. Carmel took place, the Israelites repented and Elijah slew the prophets of Baal. Then it was time for rain. Elijah prayed and it rained.

We don't always know what God wants to do through the weather, but I want you to know that there are times, and you may face them, when stormy weather will be how the enemy wants to do his work. It is then I pray you will remember the God who stilled the storm and that you will not fail to pray for a miraculous intervention in the forces of nature in order to complete the work of God.

Respect the authority of God over demons and the powers of darkness

"And He said to them, 'Begone!' And they came out, and went into the swine, and behold, the whole herd rushed down the steep bank into the sea and perished in the waters." Matthew 8:32

We recently completed a study on spiritual warfare and the person of Satan. We came away armed with this truth: no demon, no force of darkness can prevail against the prayers of Christians. Don't be afraid. Don't recoil from the opportunity. Exercise the authority given to you by God Almighty to send evil forces fleeing.

Respect the authority of God over life and death

"...Alas, who can live except God has ordained it?" Num. 24:23b "...And in Thy book they were all written, the days that were ordained for me, when as yet there was not one of them." Psalm 139:16b "He began to say, 'Depart; for

the girl has not died, but is asleep.' And they began laughing at Him. But when the crowd had been put out, He entered and took her by the hand; and the girl arose. And this news went out into all that land." Matthew 9:24-26 "Then Jesus therefore said to them plainly, 'Lazarus is dead', and when He had said these things, He cried out with a loud voice, 'Lazarus, come forth.'" John 11:14,43

Respect the authority of God over sickness and disease

*"And Jesus was going about all the cities and the villages, teaching in their synagogues, and proclaiming the gospel of the kingdom, and healing every kind of disease and every kind of sickness." Matthew 9:35 "'For this reason I did not even consider myself worthy to come to You, **but just say the word**, and my servant will be healed. For I, too, am a man under authority, with soldiers under me; and I say to this one, "Go!" and he goes; and to another, "Come!" and he comes; and to my slave, "Do this!" and he does it.' Now when Jesus heard this, He marveled at him, and turned and said to the multitude that was following Him, 'I say to you, not even in Israel have I found such great faith.'" Luke 7:7-9*

Respect the authority of God over childbirth

The more we learn about God's authority, the more He wants to reveal NEW areas of His Lordship. When doing a Bible study in Genesis, I realized that God has authority over childbirth.

*"Then Jacob's anger burned against Rachel, and he said, 'Am I in the place of God, **who has withheld from you the fruit of the womb?**'" Genesis 30:2 "Then God remembered Rachel, and **God gave heed to her and opened her womb.**" Genesis 30:22 "But he said to me, '**Behold, you***

shall conceive and give birth to a son*, and now you shall not drink wine or strong drink nor eat any unclean thing, for the boy shall be a Nazarite to God from the womb to the day of his death.'" Judges 13:7 "But to Hannah he would give a double portion, for he loved Hannah, **but the Lord had closed her womb**." I Samuel 1:5 "Her rival, however, would provoke her bitterly to irritate her, **because the Lord had closed her womb**. I Samuel 1:6 "And Isaac prayed to the Lord on behalf of his wife, because she was barren; and the Lord answered him and Rachel his wife conceived." Genesis 25:21*

I wish I had been taught this truth BEFORE I was taught about birth control. I am not against people using contraceptives, BUT if we really understood the authority of God over this particular area we could learn to trust Him in an area that now we want to control ourselves. It is control, not trust, that tells God how many children you think you can handle. It is manipulation, not yieldedness that wants to determine when you have children. I do find it a little amusing that our second child, Mary, was conceived while I was on "the pill." I kept thinking I had the flu and was three months pregnant before we even knew she was coming. I am so glad that the Lord exerted His authority over our limited understanding. I can't picture life without our sweet Mary and the joy she and her sister, Beth, have added to our lives.

Epilogue

I hope (and pray) that by pulling back the curtain on my life, and giving you a view of my spiritual journey, you will be encouraged to join me at the window of deeper prayer. As you can clearly see, through my failings, and *by His grace* some wonderful answers to prayer, God delights in using ping pong balls like you and me. These lessons are not exhaustive. As you seek to pray more, the Holy Spirit will urge you to acquire new tools in prayer every day.

    Please write and tell me some of the ways God has encouraged you in the adventure of learning more about hearing His voice. Who knows? Your stories may end up in the NEXT BOOK. You can find more in-depth Bible studies on the topics discussed in this book (with their full verse content) and others at our web site: http://www.oliveleaf-publications.com

Together, let's give the enemy some trouble today!

Suggested Authors For Further Reading

E.M. Bounds
R.A. Torrey
George Mueller
Wesley Deuwel

www.ingramcontent.com/pod-product-compliance
Lightning Source LLC
Chambersburg PA
CBHW031642170426
43195CB00035B/369